THE INTERRELATION
OF THE GREAT AWAKENING
AND HARVARD COLLEGE

THE INTERRELATION OF THE GREAT AWAKENING AND HARVARD COLLEGE

RELIGION AND LAW SERIES, VOLUME EIGHT

George J. Gatgounis

WIPF & STOCK · Eugene, Oregon

THE INTERRELATION OF THE GREAT AWAKENING
AND HARVARD COLLEGE

Religion and Law Series, Volume Eight

Copyright © 2022 George J. Gatgounis. All rights reserved. Except for brief quotations in critical publications or reviews, no part of this book may be reproduced in any manner without prior written permission from the publisher. Write: Permissions, Wipf and Stock Publishers, 199 W. 8th Ave., Suite 3, Eugene, OR 97401.

Wipf & Stock
An Imprint of Wipf and Stock Publishers
199 W. 8th Ave., Suite 3
Eugene, OR 97401

www.wipfandstock.com

PAPERBACK ISBN: 978-1-6667-5945-7
HARDCOVER ISBN: 978-1-6667-5946-4
EBOOK ISBN: 978-1-6667-5947-1

VERSION NUMBER 100622

To Professor Angela Carmella at Harvard,
who illumined me on religious evolution

CONTENTS

INTRODUCTION | 1
  Scope and Statement of Thesis | 2
    Delimitations | 2

THE GREAT AWAKENING AND HARVARD COLLEGE: THE THEOLOGICAL DIMENSION OF THEIR INTERRELATION | 3
  Harvard College's Theological Underpinnings | 3
    The Theological Aura Imbibed from the Original New England Colonists | 3
      A Binding Sense of a Common Divine Call | 4
      A Binding Sense of a Common, Newly Inaugurated Covenant | 5
      A Sense of Theological Continuity | 5
    The Eschatological Hope for Future "Latter-Day" Glory | 6
      Prescript: Eschatological Hope a Ground of the Puritan Experiment | 6
      Postscript: Eschatological Hope of Latter-Day Glory after the Death of Whitefield | 7
  Evangelical and Non-Evangelical Polarization Before the Great Awakening | 9
    The Half-Way Covenant | 9
    The "Reforming Synod" of 1679 | 10
      The Move toward Presbyterianism as a Solution to Religious Decline | 10

  Harvard's Reaction | 12
  Reaction through Jeremiads | 13
  The Conservatives' Move to Establish Another New Light, Orthodox Harvard: The Founding of Yale in 1700-1701 | 15
   Unorthodoxy in Boston Motivating a Move to Establish Another Calvinistic Bastion | 15
   Networking Among Evangelical Ministers on Both Sides of the Atlantic | 16
   Latent Unitarianism During the Mid-Eighteenth Century | 17
   The Harvard Library's Inclusion of Heterodox Material | 18
  Evangelical and Non-Evangelical Polarization During the Great Awakening | 19
   Polarization as Early as 1735 | 19
  The Advent of So-Called "Enthusiasm" in the Great Awakening | 20
   Edwards' Role in the Awakening Before the Advent of Whitefield | 20
    While Edwards Pincered the New Stirrings, Harvard Remained Cautiously Aloof | 20
    Edwards' Handling of the New Emotion Stirred by the Awakening | 20
    The Advent of Whitefield | 22
   "Enthusiasm" and Harvard College Juxtaposed | 22
    Enthusiasm Versus the Current Established Institutional Learning | 22
   Enthusiasm Opposed by the Harvard Leadership | 24
    An Example of a Balance of Godliness and Learning Enjoined at Harvard | 24
    Personal Associations of President Holyoke: Evangelical and Non Evangelical | 25
  Conclusion | 25

THE INTERRELATION OF HARVARD AND THE GREAT AWAKENING: THE LEGAL PERSPECTIVE | 27
  Legal Beginnings of the Bay Colony | 27

Legislation Aimed at Control of the Clergy Through Control of Both Harvard and Yale | 28
Connecticut's General Assembly Legislating to Dampen the Revival | 28
An Example of New Light Dissent, Legal Repression, and Eventual Autonomy | 29
One Harvard Attorney's Plea for Lockean Religious Toleration | 30
Conclusion | 30

THE GREAT AWAKENING AND HARVARD COLLEGE: THE SOCIOLOGICAL DIMENSION OF THEIR INTERRELATION | 31
The Cohesive Social Order Established by Puritan Law | 31
The Great Awakening as the First Major Outbreak of Religious Dissent | 32
Sectarianism: New to New England | 32
Miller's View of a Socio-Political Reason for Polarization | 33
Socioeconomic Perspective | 33
A "Perestroika" of the Social Order | 33
The New Wave of "Awakened" Ministers | 35
Harvard's Polarization Against the New Wave | 36
Harvard at First Brushed by the Great Awakening | 36
Whitefield's Judgment of Harvard in 1741 | 39
Charles Chauncy's Sermon against Enthusiasm One Week after Harvard's 1742 Commencement the Catalyst for Polarization | 40
Harvard's Denunciation of Whitefield in 1744 | 41
Harvard Producing the Far-Left Wing of the Polarization against the Awakening | 44
Conclusion | 45

FINAL CONCLUSION | 47

Appendix A: Mayflower Compact: 1620: Agreement between the Settlers at New Plymouth | 49

Appendix B: The Charter of Massachusetts Bay: 1629 | 51

Appendix C: Inscription from 1642 Letter
on the Founding of Harvard | 73

Appendix D: Student Rules from 1642 Letter
on the Founding of Harvard | 74

Appendix E: Laws of the Massachusetts Bay Colony 1648 | 76

Appendix F: Transcription of the Charter of 1650 | 102

Appendix G: Harvard Motto 1692 | 106

Appendix H: The Laws of Harvard College (1767) | 107

Appendix I: Harvard President Samuel Langdon 1775 | 110

Bibliography | 113

INTRODUCTION

Protruding in the history of colonial America is the religious phenomenon called "the Great Awakening." This continental divide distinguishes an old order—New England under a firm clutch of scholastic but degenerating Calvinism—and a new order —a *perestroika* into a new Pietism and Evangelicalism.[1] The clearest mark of the Great Awakening's beginning is the remarkable response to Jonathan Edward's sermon "Sinners in the Hands of an Angry God" in 1735. Historians tend to view the end of the Awakening as the death of its single most driving—even seraphic—force, the evangelist George Whitefield in 1770.

The spark generated through Edwards' preaching in 1735, more than embryonic, effervesced under the Whitefieldian animus. This New England spiritual renaissance eclipsed concurrent (between 1730 and 1760) religious resurgence in Western Europe, including Germany, Holland, Switzerland, and France. Shadowing zephyrs of spiritual awakening in Protestant circles, stirrings in Roman Catholic circles, called "Quietism," appeared as an aftershock.[2] A religious flourish pinnacled on both sides of the Atlantic, especially in the circles first resurrected by the sermonizing of Whitefield, upon whose heels the two Wesleys closely followed.

---

1. Heimert and Miller, eds. *The Great Awakening*, xvi.
2. Ibid., xv.

SCOPE AND STATEMENT OF THESIS

Delimitations

The burden of this study is explication of points of contact between Harvard College and the Great Awakening, with a view of exposing the stimulus/response, point/counterpoint, and action/reaction relationship between the institution and the movement. Accordingly, a theological evaluation of mid-eighteenth-century Harvard and a theological evaluation of the Great Awakening are outside the scope of this study. Rather, this study involves description, not critique.

Thesis Stated

The Great Awakening did not engender more latitudinarian trends at Harvard College, but rather exposed and exacerbated latitudinarian fixtures already in place. The tug of war between the conservatism of the Awakening and the latitudinarianism of the College displayed itself in theological, legal, and sociological arenas.

THE GREAT AWAKENING AND HARVARD COLLEGE

The Theological Dimension of Their Interrelation

HARVARD COLLEGE'S THEOLOGICAL UNDERPINNINGS

An appreciation of the theological underpinnings of the Harvard community before the Great Awakening involves an accurate sense of the legacy of her founders and their hope of a universal "latter-day" eschatological utopia, which would commence, allegedly, in America, probably New England.

The Theological Aura Imbibed from the Original New England Colonists

The original colonists' legacy consists of a communal sense of calling, newly inaugurated covenant, and theological continuity. Although the founding vision would evolve, fragment, distort, and modify by the time of the Great Awakening, the driving ideals of the Puritan framers would never entirely extinguish.

THE INTERRELATION OF THE GREAT AWAKENING AND HARVARD

A Binding Sense of a Common Divine Call

Interweaving the Massachusetts Bay Colony was the saturating force of a sense of divine call. Hearkening to the decree of their Sovereign, they boldly embarked to where no subject of the Sovereign had gone before — an "errand in the wilderness" of the New World. After Bay colonists established their own dwellings and meeting places for worship, and provided for their common defense, they established Harvard College to train their own ministers, lest they leave to their progeny the curse of an untrained ministry. Indispensable to their spiritual and communal survival, responding to the voice of God required mouthpieces that did not distort the pristine message — learned ministers of integrity were an imperative commodity of highest priority.

Governor John Winthrop, basking in the common sense of divine calling, expressed that all are of one body in Christ, and therefore:

> All the partes[1] of this body being thus united are made so contiguous in a special relation as they must needs partake of each others' strength and infirmity, joy, and sorrowe, weale and woe . . . . This sensibleness and Sympathy of each others' Conditions will necessarily infuse into each parte a native desire and endeavour, to strengthen defend, preserve, and comfort the other.[2]

An intensity of belief, both individually and corporately, in the call of the Christian Gospel forwarded the Puritan venture.[3]

---

1. Spelling true to original.

2. Winthrop, "A Model of Christian Charity," in *Puritan Political Ideas*, 84-85.

3. Compare, for instance, the personal testimonials, such as those of Thomas Shepard—clear and forceful expressions of the sense of divine calling. Shepard, "Autobiography," in Miller and Johnson, eds., *Puritans*, II, 472.

THE THEOLOGICAL DIMENSION OF THEIR INTERRELATION

A Binding Sense of a Common, Newly Inaugurated Covenant

Governor Winthrop's sermon aboard the *Arabella*, delivered en route to the Bay, includes passages analogizing the colonists to the ancient founders of the Israelite state. Intense conviction embraced the vision of a new Israel. The colonists believed that God had extracted them out of their sordid persecuted past to implant them into a new Israel — an Eden reconquered. God, with his new bride, had inaugurated:

> more neare[4] bond of marriage ... wherein he hath taken us to be his after a most strict and peculiar manner which will make him the more Jealous of our love and obedience since he tells the people of Israel, "you only have I known of all the families of the Earth, therefore will I punish you for your Transgressions."[5]

All spiritual, social, legal, and political dimensions of life subsumed in the all-encompassing covenant. The totality of a church-state complex was bound together "by a holy covenant, for the public worship of God, and the mutual edification one of another, in the Fellowship of the Lord Jesus."[6]

A Sense of Theological Continuity

Denominational continuity characterizes the New England scene before 1740. Solid, entrenched Congregationalism rested on the prongs of state maintenance through taxation, a consolidated organization of geographical parishes, a learned clergy trained at Harvard and Yale, and a clear standard of orthodoxy articulated in the Cambridge and Saybrook Platforms. The "denominationalism" of New England was rather uniform, "solidly and irrevocably

---

4. Spelling true to original.

5. John Winthrop, "A Model of Christian Charity," in *Puritan Political Ideas*, Morgan, 91.

6. "The Cambridge Platform," in Williston Walker, *The Creeds and Platforms of Congregationalism* (New York: Charles Scribener's Sons, 1893), 205.

rooted in the doctrines of Calvinism classically expressed in the Westminster Confession of Faith."[7]

The Eschatological Hope for Future "Latter-Day" Glory

Prescript: Eschatological Hope a Ground of the Puritan Experiment

An early work commonly read by the New England divines was John White's *The Planter's Plea* (1630). In this work, White explained that the dispersion of God's people results in the carrying of the Gospel into the whole world, so that all quarters of the earth might sound with God's praise. According to White, a consensus of the great men of the Church believe that God's scheme for the propagation of religion from the beginning "falles[8] in this last age, upon the Westerne parts of the world."[9]

White's conclusion, even phraseology, is reminiscent of Bartholomew Keckermann of Danzig's work *Manuductio to Theologie* (1621), a Protestant effort to systematize the arts and sciences into compendia acceptable to Puritan scholars, which resulted in its use as a textbook for Harvard College students. In 1624 T. Vickars translated the work into English, which included a variety of interpretations of providence, including the view that the English running second to the Spanish was God's plan, because a "little popish light" here and there prepared the way for "further truths," the full light of Puritanism, as led by "true and faithful Ministers of the Gospel." *Manuductio* predicted that "toward the end of the world the true religion shall be in America" so that Christ's prophecies of latter-day glory will be fulfilled.[10]

---

7. Stephen A. Marini, *Radical Sects of Revolutionary New England* (Cambridge: Harvard University Press, 1982), 4.

8. Spelling true to original.

9. White, *The Planter's Pea*, 65, 18.

10. White, 5-6, 12; *cf.* John Cotton, *God's Promise*, 19-20.

THE THEOLOGICAL DIMENSION OF THEIR INTERRELATION

Postscript: Eschatological Hope of Latter-Day Glory after the Death of Whitefield

The vision of eschatological utopia did not diminish after the revival fires died down to a simmer, however. The hope of latter-day glory would persist after the theological polarization sparred by the revival's stirrings. Samuel Hopkins,[11] for instance, a student of Edwards', begins his *Treatise on the Millennium* (1793) with the words "to the People who shall live in the Days of the Millennium, hail, ye happy people, highly favoured of the Lord!"[12]

Harvard graduate the Rev. Charles Coffin (class of 1793), wrote a letter in 1793 arguing for the vision of New England Christianity as the New Israel on an errand into the wilderness. Because of the rise of international commerce, Coffin emphasized that New England was founded not for commerce but for religion. Further, he argues for Edwards' view that revivals are the chief mechanism by which God advances his redemptive purposes and are thus the key to church history. Accordingly, Coffin articulated a vision of light at the end of the wilderness tunnel:

> The American church should realize her duty, till a pure and general revival shall spread its blessing over the inhabited globe. Never was there any other country settled, since Canaan itself, so much for the sacred purposes of religion, as our own. Never did any other ancestry, since the days of inspiration, send up so many prayers and lay such ample foundations for the religious prosperity of their descendants, as did our godly forefathers. It is a fact, therefore, in perfect analogy with the course of

---

11. Hopkinsianism "taught men that they were to repent; that that was their first and only duty; that they could do it of themselves and ought to do it of themselves, and that nothing else was of any avail for their salvation. It taught the use of means to effect repentance was simply deferring a duty and provoking the truth and the influence of the Holy Spirit, but were simply to repent." George Nye Boardman, "A History of New England Theology," in Kuklick, *American Religious Thought*, 216.

12. Hopkins, *A Treatise on the Millennium*, A2.

Providence, that there never has been any other country so distinguished for religious revivals as our own.[13]

Coffin believed that revivals, sprouting on American soil, would eventually spread their boughs over all the earth. America would become a Christian republic first, then other countries would follow suit:

> Our Bible, missionary education, Sabbath-school, temperance and colonization societies, the supply of our own people with a sufficient number of able and faithful ministers of the New Testament and with pious and benevolent characters for the thousand other spheres of responsible action, the diffusion of the light of life, and the joys of the gospel salvation, throughout all our numerous habitations; the preservation of our invaluable liberties and free institutions and all the happy prospects of our most favored country, depend greatly on God and upon those pure and recent spreading revivals of religion, for which all American Christians, of whatever name, should pray and labor and strive and live, with one heart and one soul; and, so far as they possess the mind and spirit of their Master, most certainly will.[14]

Revival therefore, was to most in the New England Christian community not a self-contained, "here today, gone tomorrow" phenomenon, but rather a stepping stone to higher, wider, and deeper religiosity—a Christian religiosity that would engulf the whole earth.

---

13. Coffin to Sprague, 22 July 1833, in Sprague, *Lectures on Revivals*, 399-400; Crawford, *Seasons of Grace*, 249.

14. Sprague, *Lectures*, 399-400; Crawford, *Seasons of Grace*, 249-50; *cf.* Joseph Bellamy, *The Millennium*

THE THEOLOGICAL DIMENSION OF THEIR INTERRELATION

EVANGELICAL AND NON-EVANGELICAL POLARIZATION BEFORE THE GREAT AWAKENING

The Half-Way Covenant

In 1657 thirteen teaching elders with four delegates from Connecticut joined to address the problem of an unregenerate second generation. They adopted for a solution the same mode used in the Old World—the Half-Way Covenant, allowing unregenerate parents to have their children baptized—that is, to hold visible church membership without the right to celebrate communion.[15] Conservatives at the time of the Half-Way Covenant opposed the compromise measure, among them Charles Chauncy, President of Harvard.[16]

Later conservatives after the Half-Way Covenant, however, in the eighteenth century, would support the measure. In defense of the "Half-Way" measure, Moses Hemmenway, who graduated from Harvard in 1755, wrote in 1767 Seven Sermons on the Obligation and Encouragement of the Unregenerate to Labour for the Meat Which Endureth to Everlasting Life." This brisk series begged the unconverted to expose themselves to the things of God, in anticipation of their conversion, in the context of the Half-Way Covenant. The result of this series of sermons included an increase of attendance by the unconverted to the means of grace.[17] In a similar vein, Joseph Bellamy, Jonathan Edwards' most devoted pupil, would defend the Half-Way or "external" covenant in 1769.[18]

---

15. Boardman, *A History of New England Theology*, p. 12.

16. Grandfather of Charles Chauncy, Pastor of Brattle Street Church, Boston, mid-eighteenth century.

17. Foster, *A Genetic History of the New England Theology*, 146.

18. Bellamy, *Half-Way Covenant*. And for another defense of the external covenant, see Bellamy, *A Careful and Strict Examination of the External Covenant*.

THE INTERRELATION OF THE GREAT AWAKENING AND HARVARD

The "Reforming Synod" of 1679

The Move toward Presbyterianism as a Solution to Religious Decline

The historical line between Puritan Congregationalism and Puritan Presbyterianism is not always bright—at times it is blurred, even dotted. Generally, Congregationalists distinguished themselves by allowing congregations to choose their own ministers, own their own property, and decide on frequency of synodical meetings. Conversely, Presbyterians usually (but not always) allowed the presbyteries to choose ministers for their congregations and presbyteries to own the local assemblies' property. Further, Presbyterians practiced regular meetings of presbyterial and synodical governing bodies "for the better government of the church."

Doctrinally, the two traditions tightly parallel. In 1648, for instance, the New England Congregationalists approved the Westminster Confession of Faith in Cambridge, Massachusetts. Congregationalists in England modified the Confession at the Savoy Palace in London in 1658, the New England Congregationalists following suit in 1680. In 1708, the Synod of Saybrook in Connecticut approved the Boston Confession of 1680, and provided that the Connecticut churches be governed by "consociations" comprised of ministers and "messengers" of the churches.[19]

Although a Congregationalist, Increase Mather, President of Harvard from 1685 to 1701, argued for presbyterial bodies of "consociations to meet at regular times." Mather, in his work *The First Principles of New-England*, cites John Cotten:

> that the elders and brethren of the churches, would meet together in convenient Numbers, at Set Times, (which may be left unto the Wisdom of each Society of the Churches) and thus to enjoy and practice Church-Communion. And there are added many Directions elaborated by him for the most edifying Management of such stated Councils.

---

19. Pope, *New England Calvinism*, 5.

Mather therefore did not object to the regular gathering of councils comprised of representative elders of particular assemblies.[20] Mather commends a "constant Actual Communion of the Churches within the Limits of the same Supreme Civil Government, in Councils." Citing John Owen to substantiate, Mather quotes Owen's treatise on a Gospel Church:

> I cannot see how any other of their Rights, which they hold by Divine Institution, if through more constant Lesser Synods for Advice, there be a Communication of their mutual Concerns, unto those that are Greater, until Occasion require, and it be expedient, there be a General Assembly of them all, to advise about anything wherein they are, all concerned.

To Mather, the stated councils should consist of ministers and elected delegates, "chosen once a year at least," for the purpose of consulting and advising "upon such affairs as might be a proper matter for the consideration of an ecclesiastical council."[21] Mather proposed council meetings at least per annum.[22]

As perceived moral decline intensified, Congregationalist conservatives, posturing themselves as centrists, desired expanded executive power to bring the deteriorating fringe into line. The "Reforming Synod" of 1679 in Boston, for instance, addressed itself to problems of spiritual decline but was largely ignored. Convening in 1679, the "Reforming Synod" enumerated the judgments God was inflicting on New England because of its sins:

> Heavy calamities by sea and shore, shipwrecks, droughts, conflagrations, fightings, pestilential sicknesses, and commercial disasters. These evils are considered as punishments for abounding pride, neglect of church-fellowship and other divine institutions, oaths and imprecations in ordinary discourse, Sabbath-breaking, remissness in family government and family worship,

---

20. Increase Mather, *A Faithful Account of the Discipline Professed and Practiced in the Church of New-England*, 181-82.

21. Mather, 183.

22. Mather, 184.

intemperance, promise-breaking, immodest dress and mixed dancing.[23]

The same concerns led to the Proposals of 1705, which included the effort for greater interchurch discipline among "Consociated Churches."[24]

Harvard's Reaction

A more latitudinarian faction, centering around Harvard, successfully thwarted a coup de l'église of "Consociated Churches" moving toward greater central executive authority to discipline error. The conservative faction of Congregationalists, moving toward Presbyterianism, urged the particular churches "in all holy Watchfulness and helpfulness towards each other" to withdraw communion from a church that refuses to be healed of "such gross disorders as plainly hurt the common Interest."[25] Harvard's influence in 1679 weighed against the presbyterial remedy to heteropraxis. Harvard's reaction, however, may not have derived solely or even primarily from infidelity. Rather, the Harvard establishment maintained a stringent fear of ecclesiastical tyranny.

Both those in government and friends of Harvard College were alarmed, for instance, about the design of some of the Episcopal church to obtain official influence in the institution's concerns.[26] The Episcopal Society for Propagating the Gospel in Foreign Parts established a mission and set up a church in Cambridge, approximately a quarter mile from the College. Various clergy in the area viewed the encroachment as a "formal design to carry on a spiritual siege of our churches, with the hope that they will one day submit to a spiritual sovereign."[27] To remaining first-generation Puritans, still with the bitter taste of ecclesiastical

---

23. Boardman, *A History of New England Theology*, 20.
24. Gaustad, *The Great Awakening*, 13.
25. Ibid.
26. Quincy, 2:74.
27. Mayhew, *A Defence*, 56, 67.

tyranny in their mouths, a return to "top-down" ecclesiastical bureaucracies was ghastly unthinkable.

Reaction through Jeremiads

As Puritan ministers perceived intensifying and accelerating moral and theological declension, they resorted to the homiletic device of a jeremiad, a sermon calling the populace back to God in the manner and spirit of the prophet Jeremiah (cf. ch. 7).[28] At the inception of the colony, ministers were not only, so to speak, on the playing field, but were quarterbacking. As time passed, their centrality dimmed to be societally somewhat like those coaching from the sidelines. Their hegemony, however, continued to spiral downward to where they were relegated to an honored front row at the fifty-yard line. They would eventually, in the later generations, be consigned to the back row. Perhaps the day would come when they were not allowed into the stadium at all. The jeremiad became not only a plea for change of belief and behavior among the people, but a social restructuring device, where the ministers made their case of why the colony would be better served with them at its helm.

Increase Mather, president of Harvard from 1685 to 1701, for instance, in 1678 lamented the degeneration of the people's morals: "the body of the rising generation is a poor, perishing, unconverted and (except the Lord pour down his spirit) undone generation!"[29] Mather saw that the time of trouble for New England was near, as testified by a variety of signs, including "great security" among

---

28. Joseph Bellamy, A blow at the root of the refined antinomianism of the present age. Wherein that maxim, which is so absolutely essential to their scheme, that it cannot subsist without it, laid down by Mr. Marshall, viz. That in justifying faith, "we believe that to be true, which is not true before we believe it," thoroughly examined: Mr. Wilson's arguments in its defence, considered and answered; and the whole antinomian controversy, as it now stands, brought to a short issue, rendered plain to the meanest capacity (Boston: S. Kneeland, in Queen-Street, M, DCC, LXIII [1763]).

29. Dexter, *The Congregationalism of the Last Three Hundred Years*, 476.

the people: "you are asleep and your Judgment is slumbering too, when as it's waiting ready to take hold of you."[30]

Mather pulled no punches: "the present Generation in New-England is lamentably degenerate. As sometimes Moses spake to the Children of Israel, Numb. 32:14. 'Behold ye are risen up in your Fathers stead an increase of sinful men.' So may we say, the first Generation of Christians in New-England, in a manner gone off the Stage, and there is another more sinful Generation risen up in their stead."[31] Mather underscored his declamation: "It is an apt similitude which some use, that as the heat of the Sun in Summer breeds a multitude of Insects, so doth the warmth of prosperity a multitude of apostates."[32] For correction, Mather urged reformation of the particular sins of the day:

> ... in order to Serving our Generation, we should consider what are the Special Sins of the Age wherein we Live, and Endeavour the Reformation of them; and what are the more peculiar Truths and Duties of the Times, so as to fall in them. There are some Evils which are *Errores Seculi*, the more special Errors of that Age, either Practical or Doctrinal: Sometimes one Evil breaks forth, sometimes another. As any Scandal appears, we shall do a good Service in our Generation, to give a faithful Testimony against it, if it be indeed a Sin.[33]

Summarily, jeremiads were, from the conservatives' perspective, the colony's last best hope.

---

30. Mather, "The Day of Trouble Is Near," Sacvan Bercovitch, ed., *Jeremiads: A Library of American Puritan Writings*, 8.
31. Mather in *Jeremiads*, 61.
32. Ibid.
33. Mather in *Jeremiads*, 17.

THE THEOLOGICAL DIMENSION OF THEIR INTERRELATION

The Conservatives' Move to Establish Another New Light, Orthodox Harvard: The Founding of Yale in 1700-1701

Unorthodoxy in Boston Motivating a Move to Establish Another Calvinistic Bastion

The traditional Calvinistic leaders at the turn of the century, alarmed that the parties of most powerful influence favored the new winds blowing, looked away from Boston to establish a new academic bastion of Calvinistic faith in 1700-1701.[34] As the years passed, so did the liberalizing tendencies. As a result, in the year 1752, the clergy of Connecticut, with the Calvinistic sect in Massachusetts, sedulously began the task[35] of "settling and securing orthodoxy in the College of New Haven, and to preserve it, in all the governors thereof, upon the best foundation that human wisdom, directed by the general rules of God's word, could devise."[36] In November 1753, the President and Fellows of Yale voted for strict orthodox observance:

> [T]he students should be established in the principles of religion, according to the Assembly's Catechism, Dr. Ames' 'Medulla' and 'Cases of Conscience,' and should not be suffered to be instructed in any different principles or doctrines ... that the Assembly's Catechism, and the Confession of Faith, received and established in the churches of this colony, (which is an abridgment of the Westminster Confession,) contain a true and just summary of the most important doctrines of the Christian religion, and that the true sense of the sacred Scriptures is justly collected and summed up, in these positions, and all expositions of Scripture pretending to deduce any doctrines or positions contrary to the doctrines laid down in these composures, we are of the opinion, are wrong and erroneous; and that every President, Fellow, Professor of Divinity, or Tutor in said College shall, before he enter upon the execution of his office, publicly

---

34. Quincy, 2:70.
35. Ibid.
36. Clap, *The Annals or History of Yale-College*, 75.

consent to the said Catechism and Confession of Faith, as containing a just summary of the Christian religion, and renounce all doctrines and principles contrary thereto, and shall pass through such examination, as the Corporation shall think proper, in order to their being fully satisfied that he should do it truly, and without any evasion or equivocation.[37]

The year after the resolution the number of students acceding to Yale exceeded those attending Harvard, the number being viewed as a providential smile upon the undertaking, that strict adherence to Calvinistic doctrine was the path to prosperity.[38]

Networking Among Evangelical Ministers on Both Sides of the Atlantic

Early eighteenth-century networking of evangelically oriented ministers, as opposed to those tending to liberalize, included circles in the colonies and Britain.[39] J. Nelson quips in regard to the evangelicals' cohesion, "evangelicals ... found their gushing fount of authority in the Bible, and they made little of creeds." Isaac Watts and Benjamin Colman, for instance, became an axis of networking for evangelically oriented ministers on both sides of the Atlantic in the 1720s. Watts' poems, sermons, and hymns were studied at Harvard and Yale, where Edwards was among those who masticated Watts' contributions. Colman (1673-1747) spent the late 1690s in England, then served as the original pastor of Boston's Brattle Street Church, although the liberal membership at the Brattle church distressed the Mathers. Colman, in gratitude to English dissenting evangelical Thomas Hollis, dedicated to him a series of discourses called "Some Glories of Our Lord and Savior Jesus Christ."[40] Through the introduction of Cotton Mather, Robert Wodrow and Colman maintained steady correspondence on

37. Clap, The Annals or History of Yale-College, 62.
38. Quincy, 2:71.
39. Nelson, The Rise of the Princeton Theology, 155.
40. Crawford, Seasons of Grace, 68.

the decay of religion in Scotland and New England, respectively. Wodrow also communicated with friends of Colman, including Edward Wigglesworth, Hollis Professor at Harvard College, as well as eight or nine ministers in his neighborhood.[41]

Latent Unitarianism During the Mid-Eighteenth Century

Unitarianism, though latent in the early eighteenth century, was not openly professed or publicly advocated in New England during the mid-eighteenth century. The appearance of Samuel Mather's tract of 1718, "Necessity of Believing the Doctrine of the Trinity" implies, however, the latent growth of Unitarianism. In 1758 Joseph Bellamy printed an exegetical treatise, Treatise on the Divinity of Christ,[42] and in 1768 Hopkins preached a sermon defending the divinity of Christ, "under a conviction that the doctrine was much neglected, if not disbelieved by a number of ministers in Boston."[43]

Modern Socinian or Unitarians were actually the ancient Ebionites, Samosatenians, Sabellians, Arians, or Photians resurrected.[44] Among the foremost of forerunners of New England's nineteenth-century Unitarian/Universalism was Charles Chauncy (d. 1792), grandson of a Harvard president. Breaking with "Old Calvinism," Chauncy later "rejected eternal damnation," acknowledging that everyone would be saved.[45] Although Jonathan

---

41. Crawford, 69.

42. Bellamy's pedagogy involved giving students a list of his questions on principal subjects of theology and directing them to read the best theological treatises. During the evenings, Bellamy would examine his students individually on their views. Topics included the existence, attributes, and government of God, the law, the sinful state and character of mankind, divine revelation, gospel doctrines, the character and offices of Christ, the atonement, regeneration, justification, repentance, Christian graces, perseverance of the saints, resurrection and final judgment, heaven and hell, the church, its natures, offices, ordinances, and discipline. Leonard Woods, History of the Andover Theological Seminary (Boston: James R. Osgood, 1885), 19-20.

43. Foster, *A Genetic History of the New England Theology*, 274.

44. Wilbur, *A History of Unitarianism*, 8.

45. Bruce Kuklick, *Churchmen and Philosophers: From Jonathan Edwards*

Mayhew died in 1766, some twenty years before Chauncy, Mayhew had voiced the "nub of Boston's discontent with Connecticut and western Massachusetts orthodoxy: a disbelief in the divinity of Christ and an emphasis on the supreme and benign glory of God the Father," to the denuding of the doctrine of His wrath.[46]

The Harvard Library's Inclusion of Heterodox Material

By the time of Whitefield's arrival, the Harvard library contained the works largely held responsible for ever-enlarging liberalization—Locke, Newton, Clarke, Sydney, Milton, Butler, even Hutcheson and Priestly.[47] By as early as 1772, President Locke of Harvard argued that "foreign errors are to be met with argument alone, not by crowding down creeds and confessions upon the pain of eternal punishment."[48] Responding with alacrity, Jedidiah Morse (1761-1826), aggrieved with Harvard College, declaimed against her:

> It is no longer what it once was . . . . The lustre[49] of science still shines, but the Sun of Christianity is eclipsed. Young men leave the place now, not with hosannas in their mouths to the Son of David; but with burning zeal to propagate the new philosophy. Does the parent who bows the knee to Jesus, wish his son to deny the Lord that bought him? If not, let him well reflect what destination he gives him, to be taught the principles of religion as well as science.[50]

In contradistinction to later tolerances, Harvard's past resistance against erroneous theology evidenced its fervor from time to

---

to *John Dewey* (New Haven: Yale University Press, 1985), 78.
46. Kuklick, 80.
47. Haroutunian, *The Passing of the New England Theology*, 179.
48. Allen, *The Unitarian Movement Since the Reformation*, 180-81.
49. Spelling true to original.
50. Morse, *Review of American Unitarianism*, 19.

time in presidential book burnings. The last[51] presidential bonfire of books occurred in 1699, under Mather's presidency, of the half vellum octavo *More Wonders of the Invisible World*.[52] Presidential book burnings included a fanfare of imprecatory prayer.

EVANGELICAL AND NON-EVANGELICAL POLARIZATION DURING THE GREAT AWAKENING

Polarization as Early as 1735

Although the revival of 1735 was of brief duration, party lines developed into "old lights" and "new lights"—those who would wait for the effect of the means of grace, and those who would take the kingdom of God by violence (*cf.* Matt. 11:12).[53] The number of converts in the revival of 1740 numbered in the thousands, perhaps as high as twenty-five, or even fifty, thousand.[54] Fueling the evangelical side of the polarization were "new light" itinerants, which included Edwards and Joseph Bellamy, who itinerated during 1741 and later, being invited to preach in various towns.[55]

---

51. The early Presidents of Harvard include Nathaniel Eaton (Master) (1637-39), Henry Dunster (1640-54), Charles Chauncy (1654-72), Leonard Hoar (1772-75), Urian Oakes (1675-81), John Rogers (1682-84), Increase Mather (1685-1701), and Samuel Willard (Vice-President) (1701-1707). Williams Ames, author of the influential *Marrow of Divinity*, would probably have been the first President had he not died in the Netherlands, prior to embarking to the New World.

52. Alfred K. Moe, *A History of Harvard* (Cambridge, Mass.: 1896), 41.

53. George Nye Boardman in Kuklick, ed. *American Religious Thought of the 18th and 19th Centuries*, 1987), 36.

54. Ibid.

55. Ibid.

THE ADVENT OF SO-CALLED "ENTHUSIASM" IN THE GREAT AWAKENING

Edwards' Role in the Awakening Before the Advent of Whitefield

While Edwards Pincered the New Stirrings, Harvard Remained Cautiously Aloof

Revival fires burned with greater or less intensity until the first visit of Whitefield in 1740.[56] What Edwards called "revivals" and "extraordinary awakenings," Josiah Quincy, a Harvard historian, calls "excitements."[57] According to Edwards, the Awakening was "the most remarkable outpouring of the Spirit of God, that has ever been in New England, and it may be, in the world, since the days of the Apostles."[58] Edwards and the clergy of his party curbed the passions of the city folk, ignited by the revival preaching, into the limits they deemed safe and Scriptural. They realized however that it was far more easy to enkindle and spread a flame than to quench or control it.[59] Harvard College, pulled into the vortex of the theological controversies resulting from the initial stirrings, faced the new religious forces with cautious aloofness.[60]

Edwards' Handling of the New Emotion Stirred by the Awakening

Edwards did not attempt to cast a damper on the fire he attempted to kindle, but clarified that times when the "influences of the Spirit of God abound, are those in which counterfeits also abound ... the Devil being then abundant in mimicking both the ordinary and

---

56. Josiah Quincy, *A History of Harvard University*, 2:58.
57. Quincy, 2:58.
58. *Works of President Edwards*, Vol. VII, 153.
59. Quincy, 2:59.
60. *Cf.* 2:59

THE THEOLOGICAL DIMENSION OF THEIR INTERRELATION

extraordinary influences of that Spirit."[61] Edwards explained that revival cycles in a twofold modality—a proactive movement of God with a reactive response from Satan:

> the same persons may be the subjects of much of the influences of the Spirit of God, and yet in some things be led away by the delusions of the Devil; and that this is no more of a paradox than many other things that are true of real saints, in the present state, where grace dwells with so much corruption, and the new man and the old subsist together in the same person, and the kingdom of God and kingdom of the Devil remain for a while together in the same heart.[62]

One of the friends of Edwards, William Cooper, a clergyman of distinction in Boston, published Edwards' discourse, "The Distinguishing Marks of a Work of the Spirit of God," with a preface of his own, viewing the Awakening in glowing terms, and remarked that the stirrings are

> so wonderful, as that the like had not been since the pouring out of the Spirit, immediately after our Lords' ascension. The apostolical times seem to have returned upon us, such a display has there been of the power and grace of the divine Spirit in the assemblies of his people.[63]

Cooper interpreted the "prejudices and reproaches cast on this work of God" as the "raging of Satan when his kingdom is shaken, and his subjects desert him."[64] By championing revival, however, Edwards at the same time upheld and broke down the traditional Puritan ecclesiastical/political complex because his advocacy polarized "pro" and "anti" factions.[65]

---

61. "The Distinguishing Marks of a Work of the Spirit of God," a Discourse delivered at New Haven, September 10th, 1741 (Boston Edition, 1741), 2.
62. Ibid., 33.
63. Quincy, *A History of Harvard*, 2:60.
64. Quincy, 2:60-61.
65. De Jong, *The Covenant Idea in New England Theology*, 143.

THE INTERRELATION OF THE GREAT AWAKENING AND HARVARD

The Advent of Whitefield

"Cambridgeites" responded with life and energy to the extemporaneous effusions of Whitefield, Edwards having prepared the field for Whitefield's labors.[66] Lay preachers began to multiply and swarm, and surpassed Whitefield in effect and zeal.[67] Whitefield was the harbinger of a new spiritual tidal wave[68]—its newness engendering a mingled response of both welcome and cautious curiosity.

"Enthusiasm" and Harvard College Juxtaposed

Enthusiasm Versus the Current Established Institutional Learning

"Enthusiasm," a derisive term of art, allegedly scoffed at scholarly preaching, "railing against learning," and encouraging "both ignorant and unlettered Men and Women to preach and teach the multitudes." The establishment believed, as expressed by Thomas Story, they must defend the status quo: "what of learning, a respect for reason, the accumulation of knowledge which God directed good Christians to utilize, even Harvard College?"[69]

Perry Miller thinks that the Great Awakening occurred in part because "common people" rose up in declaration that what Harvard and Yale were teaching was "too academic."[70] The response,

---

66. Cf. Quincy, 2:59.

67. Ibid.

68. Various works demonstrated intense missionary and evangelistic concern, such as Samuel Hopkins (1693-1755), *An address to the people of New-England. Representing the very great importance of attaching the Indians to their interest; no only by treating them justly and kindly; but by using proper endeavors to settle Christianity among them* and Jonathan Edwards, (1703-58), *The great concern of a watchman for souls, appearing in the duty he has to do, and the account he has to give, represented & improved, in a sermon preach'd at the ordination of the Reverend Mr. Jonathan Judd, to the pastoral office over the Church of Christ, in the new precinct at Northampton, June, 8, 1743.*

69. *A Journal of the Life of Thomas Story*, 340-42.

70. Heimert and Miller, eds., *The Great Awakening*, xvi.

however, may not be so much against learning per se but what they were learning, and that they were learning without the godly disciplines that had been built into Harvard from its founding in 1636. Students originally had to read the Scriptures for themselves twice a day and report on their devotional reading to a tutor or professor once a day. Waiving personal devotional requirements such as these prompted Increase Mather to call Harvard "godless Harvard" in 1692.

"Enthusiasm" Epitomized by the Quakers

Harvard College represented the belief that education and religious insight worked hand in hand, but to this belief Quakers reacted, among them George Fox, who early in his journal argued that study at Oxford and Cambridge did not fit men to be ministers of Christ. Not "Latine, Greek or Hebrew, that teacheth to understand the Scripture, but it is the Spirit of God." Quakers sought to short-circuit the path of learning Harvard represented, eliminating the intellectual baggage that bogged down orthodox people.[71] Judge Samuel Sewall, repulsed by Quakerism, declared it a rebellion against the glorious past of New England, calling it a profane heresy, even voting in city council against permitting construction of a new Quaker meeting house in Boston, testifying he "would not have a hand in setting up their Devil Worship."[72] Joseph Bellamy (1719-90), for instance, wrote a work purposed at distinguishing enthusiasm from true religion, *True Religion Delineated*.[73] Further, many in the Connecticut Valley requested for clarification of the nature of true religion, asking for publication of Joseph Bellamy's sermons "Theron, Paulinus, and Aspasio. Or, Letters and dialogues, upon the nature of love to God, faith in Christ, assurance of a title to eternal life"[74] and "An essay on the nature and glory of the Gospel of Jesus Christ: as also on the nature

---

71. Story, *Journal* 340-342.
72. Sewall, *The Diary of Samuel Sewall*, I, 6000.
73. Bellamy, *True Religion Delineated*, 1750.
74. Bellamy, *Theron, Paulinus, and Aspasio*, 1759.

and consequences of spiritual blindness: and the nature and effects of Divine illumination."[75]

Enthusiasm Opposed by the Harvard Leadership

An Example of a Balance of Godliness and Learning Enjoined at Harvard

Sarah Edwards looked askance at the response to Whitefield on the Harvard campus, writing that "the boys at Harvard, received nothing but enthusiasm from Whitefield and Tennent, along with large doses of pride and a Contempt of their Betters, despite all their holy talk."[76] (Gilbert Tennent was a New Jersey minister who admired Whitefield and sometimes traveled with him.) Thomas Story remarked to the Harvard students who gathered around him one afternoon under a "large spreading oak close to Harvard yard" that human learning could be useful but only when the "spirit of Truth" had subjected the mind. He warned them not to sin against God, by depending upon what was acquired at the "foundation of human learning," but drink rather at the "living foundation, the river of living water."[77]

Thomas Story confessed that he felt at ease among the Harvard boys, whom he found more "solid," "more like Christians," than any students he had met at Oxford or Cambridge, Edinburgh, Glasgow, or Aberdeen. His comfort was not denuded by his lecturing them on how far New England had strayed from its glorious past when the "Gifted Brethren" dominated.[78]

---

75. Bellamy, *An essay on the nature and glory of the Gospel of Jesus Christ*, 1762).

76. Sarah Edwards to James Pierrepont, Oct. 24, 1740, in Tyerman, *Life of George Whitefield*, I, 428-29; Josiah Smith, "A Sermon on the Character, Preaching, &c. of the Rev. Mr. Whitefield" (1740), in Heimert and Miller, eds. *The Great Awakening*, 67-68; Chauncy, *Seasonable Thoughts*, 51; George Whitefield, *A Vindication and Confirmation of the Remarkable Work of God in New-England*, 12.

77. Story, *Journal*, 340-342.

78. Story, 342.

THE THEOLOGICAL DIMENSION OF THEIR INTERRELATION

Personal Associations of President Holyoke: Evangelical and Non Evangelical

President Holyoke, however, appeared to play both the conservative, pro-Yale, and more liberal sides. The liberal views of Chauncy and Mayhew received no public sanction from the governors of Harvard College, but they enjoyed demonstrable friendship, professional discourse, and interchange of ministerials' labors.[79] Demonstrable "hobnobbing" between Holyoke, Chauncy, and Mayhew implies that Holyoke did not openly resist the liberalizing trends. Holyoke, however, also maintained cordial relations with evangelically oriented ministers, the Rev. Dr. Benjamin Colman, for instance. President Holyoke in a 1748 Commencement Day address dilated with eloquence on the contribution of Colman, who was then a patron to Harvard College.[80] Colman had previously been of the party of the evangelically oriented ministers who corresponded with Isaac Watts.[81]

Conclusion

By 1748 the "flame" Whitefield had raised in the colonies was about that time subsiding. As Josiah Quincy concludes, "like a fire in the woods, it had enkindled whatever was light and inflammatory, heated whatever was solid and incombustible, and began now to cease through exhaustion of the materials."[82] Harvard College, at first touched by the preaching of Whitefield, gradually hardened into a public denunciation of him, including the more extreme facets of the revival. Still steering toward center as much as she could, Harvard College never denounced Edwards, perhaps because he was a fellow New Englander, a Yale graduate, not a pure itinerant,

---

79. Quincy, 2:69.

80. Quincy, 2:77.

81. The first president of Yale was Abraham Pierson. During his presidency the rasping but lively ballad originated, "Harvard was Harvard when Yale was but a pup." Moe, *A History of Harvard*, 42.

82. Quincy, 2:77.

THE INTERRELATION OF THE GREAT AWAKENING AND HARVARD

and most pointedly, he did not publish lists of ministers he believed were unconverted.

THE INTERRELATION OF HARVARD AND THE GREAT AWAKENING

The Legal Perspective

LEGAL BEGINNINGS OF THE BAY COLONY

In 1631 the General Court for the Massachusetts Bay Colony adopted a resolution limiting voting status to church members:

> To the end the body of the Commons may be preserved of honest and good men, it is likewise preserved and agreed that for time to come, no man shall be admitted to the freedom of the body politic, but such as are members of some of the churches within the limits of the same.[1]

Palfrey called this court "the first cisatlantic General Court for election," seeing the formation of a new aristocracy of spirituality:

> They established a kind of aristocracy hitherto unknown. Not birth, nor wealth, nor learning, nor skill in war, was to confer political power, but personal character,—goodness of the highest type,—goodness of that purity and force which only the faith of Jesus Christ is competent to create.[2]

---

1. Boardman in Kuklick, *American Religious Thought*, 16.
2. Ibid.

Massachusetts enjoyed a new breed of leadership, comprised of an aristocracy of spiritual merit.

LEGISLATION AIMED AT CONTROL OF THE CLERGY THROUGH CONTROL OF BOTH HARVARD AND YALE

Church and state, still wed in New England in the mid-seventeenth century, worked as two hands washing each other to accomplish the will of whoever was in control. When opposition to the Whitefieldian revival mounted, a legal dimension of opposition solidified.

Connecticut's General Assembly Legislating to Dampen the Revival

The reaction to the Awakening included clerical discipline aimed at firmer control of the agencies of education. In Connecticut, for instance, New Light Separates were not allowed to attend the established schools; legislation prevented them from starting their own schools without a license from the state's General Assembly, which license would be denied. The same legislation stated "no Person who has not been educated or graduated at Yale College, or at Harvard College in Cambridge, or some Foreign Protestant College or University, shall be allowed the special Privileges of the established Ministers of Government."[3]

In reaction, Timothy Allen attempted to establish the "Shepherds Tent" to train ministers, which had 14 students but which expired after several months in Rhode Island.[4] Three institutions, however, successfully broached the early stormy years. Dartmouth, incorporated in 1769, was an outgrowth of New Light Eleazar Wheelock's Indian School in Lebanon, founded December 18,

---

3. Gaustad, *The Great Awakening*, 108.
4. Ibid.

1754.[5] Stirring in 1739 to found a school in New Jersey comparable to Harvard and Yale revitalized under the initiative of the pro-revivalist Presbyterian Synod of New York. The college opened at Elizabethtown in May 1747, as a direct result of the Middle Colony revival. New Light New Englanders, however, both immediate and remote, in the presbyteries of the New York Synod, which were comprised of ministers of demonstrable influence, played a key role. The College of New Jersey, or Princeton, served as a nursery for piety not only for Middle Colony Presbyterians but also New Light Congregationalists. Seventeen of its first sixty-nine graduates served as ministers in New England.[6] James Manning, member of the Princeton class of 1762, was chosen as President of New England's third college, chartered in 1764, first located at Warren, Rhode Island, which later moved to Providence in 1770, where its name was changed to Brown in 1804.[7]

An Example of New Light Dissent, Legal Repression, and Eventual Autonomy

Samuel Bird is an example of a New Light Harvard scholar whom Harvard marginalized, not allowing him to graduate. Bird preached to the church of New Haven, first called the "Tolerated Church," on May 7, 1742, because it successfully claimed the benefits of the Act of Toleration, which allowed for churches independent of the Congregationalist parish. They later chose the name "White Haven." Preaching was difficult to secure after repressive acts passed in 1742, though before the acts numerous sympathetic ministers from other churches in the environs, such as John Graham of Southbury, Joseph Bellamy of Bethlelem, Jedidah Mills of Ripton, Philemon Robbins of Branford, and Nenajah Case of Simbury, filled the pulpit. The first preacher to remain was an exhorter

5. Ibid.
6. Ibid.
7. Ibid.

from New London, John Curtis, who served from October 1748 to October 1750. Curtis, however, was never ordained.

The first ordained minister was Samuel Bird. Bird, who had been preaching at Dunstable, Massachusetts, was expelled from Harvard just before graduation in 1744 for New Light sentiments.[8] Significantly, the White Haven church achieved legal standing from the legislature in 1759, partly because it outnumbered the First Church 179 to 147. The legalization of the White Haven church was but one milestone of the beginning of the dismantling of the traditional parish pattern in Connecticut.[9]

One Harvard Attorney's Plea for Lockean Religious Toleration

Responding to the legislation of the Connecticut General Assembly, Elisha Williams (1694-1755) wrote anonymously a plea for toleration according to a Lockean apprehension of church-state relations. A graduate of Harvard, Williams first practiced law, then served on the Connecticut General Assembly, then was ordained in 1721.[10]

CONCLUSION

The tragic adage "the law is a whore" may have been the heart-cry of sincere, concerned, and activist "New Lights" in the mid-eighteenth century. Legal repression at first hampered the acceptability of "New Light" ministers by denying them the institutions of the day, Harvard and Yale. To minister unordained was gauche; to be ordained one must be "Old Light"; and to graduate, as in the case of Samuel Bird, one could be no more than a "closet New Light."

---

8. Goen, *Revivalism and Separatism in New England*, 88ff.
9. Ibid.
10. Williams, *The Essential Rights and Liberties of Protestants*, 44-53, 60-65; Heimert and Miller, *The Great Awakening*, 323.

THE GREAT AWAKENING AND HARVARD COLLEGE

The Sociological Dimension of Their Interrelation

THE COHESIVE SOCIAL ORDER ESTABLISHED BY PURITAN LAW

When the Puritans erected their "city upon a hill" in the 1620s, they established a culture somewhat distinct in social texture from that of the other colonies. Conflicting interest groups in New York and Pennsylvania, for instance, vied for their interests in the political and economic arena.[1] The southern royal colonies endured class violence and a subsistence crisis. Further, fear of the growing black population in the south solidified the white aristocracy. Social unrest, however, was rare in the Bay Colony; rather, Massachusetts was remarkably cohesive socially. Differences revolved around religious issues, such as the Half-Way Covenant, and policy concerns, such as the regulation of navigation to appease the British Crown.[2] Biblical law provided a social emulsifier for the colony. Additionally, the comprehensiveness and severity of biblical law raised the moral concerns of the colonists.

1. Pencak, *War, Politics, and Revolution in Provincial Massachusetts*, 2.
2. Ibid.

As an emulsifier, biblical law pervaded the school system in Massachusetts. Since the ideological indoctrination began at an early age for all children, the society developed an ideological commonality that bound the colony together.[3] Unlike Pennsylvania, where the Dutch Reformed taught their children in Dutch, Quakers taught their children according to their distinctives, and the Swedish Covenant churches taught their children according to their creed and in their language, only a small minority of the Massachusetts colonists differed from the Puritan creed and all spoke English.[4] Commonality in creed and language was unique to Massachusetts and Connecticut in comparison with the other colonies.

THE GREAT AWAKENING AS THE FIRST MAJOR OUTBREAK OF RELIGIOUS DISSENT

Sectarianism: New to New England

Under, however, the itinerant preaching of George Whitefield and the didactic preaching of Jonathan Edwards, the first major outbreak of religious dissent began. When the revival spread throughout New England with radical demand for spiritual rebirth, moral purity, and personal engagement with the Gospel, the new wave of the regenerate were advised by Whitefield to shun the unconverted ministers. Further, Whitefield's disciple James Davenport called the regenerate wave to come out of established Congregationalism and become a separate organization.[5]

The first native sectarian movement on New England's soil were the Separate or Strict Congregationalists led by their new Moses, James Davenport. The Separates maintained the tenets of Calvinism but incorporated the New Light revivalism. Their key distinctive included ecclesiology and discipline. The New Light Congregationalists endorsed itineracy, experiential standards for

---

3. Pencak, *War, Politics, and Revolution in Provincial Massachusetts*, 2-6.
4. Wertenbaker, *The Puritan Oligarchy*.
5. Marini, *Radical Sects of Revolutionary New England*, 4.

church membership and ministerial vocation, and sought to sever the bond of church and state. The new establishment was transient however, the nearly 100 new congregations established in the 1740s and 50s suffering an equally meteoric decline, many of the new congregations rejoining the Congregationalist establishment or becoming Baptists.[6]

MILLER'S VIEW OF A SOCIO-POLITICAL REASON FOR POLARIZATION

Socioeconomic Perspective

Socioeconomic classes existed in the Bay Colony from the earliest times; as the colony matured, class structures calcified. Not only between the "haves" and "have nots," but rifts developed between the commercialists of the port cities of Boston and Salem and farmers of the interior. Within the port city business complex, a chasm expanded between the merchant class and the small shopkeepers and artisans.[7] In Boston at around the turn of the century, "the tradition of unemotional religion became well established, and there was developing a 'free and catholic' spirit which emphasized practical morality at the same time that it maintained a gentlemanly tolerance of theological differences."[8]

A "Perestroika" of the Social Order

The dominant figures in and around Boston were the Mathers; in the Connecticut valley Solomon Stoddard was, according to Wright, "a virtual dictator."[9] The valley had come to distrust the liberalizing tendencies of Harvard, its "free and catholic tradition" exemplified by Presidents Leverett and Holyoke, Tutor

---

6. Ibid.
7. Wright, *The Beginnings of Unitarianism in America*, 31.
8. Wright, 34.
9. Wright, 33.

William Brattle, and Professor Edward Wigglesworth. No clear paradigm shift from orthodoxy had yet flagrantly occurred.[10] Charles Chauncy's virtues were, according to Wright, "the prosaic ones— diligence, sobriety, common sense, and devotion to scholarship"[11]—a primitive Boston "Brahmen."

The wake of Whitefield's preaching tended to undermine the social order both by weakening the traditional New England parish system and diminishing the prestige of established ministers.[12] Miller sees the political implications of the revival as stirring the pundits of Cambridge to such rancor. To Miller, the revival instilled a sense of individual responsibility that ran counter to the enfeebling dependence upon aristocracy, bred or earned, to govern them: "this is one thing they meant: the end of the reign over the New England and American mind of a European and scholastical conception of authority put over men because men were incapable of recognizing their own welfare." To Miller, fear fueled the anti-revivalist fervor:

> this insight may assist us somewhat in comprehending why the pundits of Boston and Cambridge, all of whom were rational and tolerant and decent, shuddered with a horror that was deeper than mere dislike of the antics of the yokels. To some extent, they sensed that the religious screaming had implications in the realm of society, and those implications they—being businessmen and speculators, as were the plutocracy of Northampton—did not like.

Accordingly, the politically entrenched, seeing the force of the revival as a potential threat to their hold on power, responded with "hysterical agony."[13]

Indeed, the revival altered the role the common person, because in the reconstitution of the churches after the revival, the

---

10. Wright, 34.
11. Wright, 36.
12. Wright, 38.
13. Heimert and Miller, *The Great Awakening*, xli; Miller, "Edwards and the Great Awakening," 8-19.

laity gained greater power, evidenced by the greater involvement in choosing ministers and assessing the spiritual character of their fellow citizens.[14] John Wesley, who would follow on the heels of Whitefield, would also mobilize laity into organizations later to become Methodist societies. Michael Harrington records that Wesley's "sober, abstemious reading of the Bible, with its stress on individual righteousness rather than collective action, had a profound impact, political as well as religious, on workers."[15]

The New Wave of "Awakened" Ministers

The ministry of Whitefield alone resulted perhaps in the ordination of as many as twenty Massachusetts ministers.[16] Sterling examples of newly converted New Light ministers include Daniel Rogers, Andrew Croswell, and Benjamen Randell. Massachusetts' most widely traveled itinerant was Daniel Rogers (brother to Nathaniel), a Harvard tutor converted under Whitefield and ordained as evangelist at large in York, Maine, in July 1742. The *Boston Evening Post* denounced the ordination of Rogers as unlawful, designating Rogers a "vagrant preacher to the people of God in this land; contrary to the peace of our Lord the King and head of his Church and of the good order and Constitution of the churches in New England as established by the platform."[17]

Andrew Croswell epitomized the New Light experiential focus. One of James Davenport's most vocal partisans, Croswell focused his ministry on the theme (more than any other) of the Christian's personal delight in knowing Christ. Commensurate in this focus is that one must know Christ particularly, not merely generally. Croswell accordingly assailed Harvard as having fallen into the pit of rationalism, a "New Divinity" which contents itself

---

14. *The Great Awakening*, lv.
15. Harrington, *The Politics at God's Funeral*, 46.
16. Goen, *Revivalism and Separatism in New England, 1740-1800*, 17.
17. Cited by Thomas Franklin Waters, *Ipswhich in The Massachusetts Bay Colony* (Ipswich, 1917), II, 122; Goen, *Revivalism and Separatism in New England*, 12.

with a mere intellectual apprehension of Christ's work for humanity in general—individual conversion through knowing Christ in particular, however, lapsed out of the new Harvard theologues' purview.[18]

The founder of the Freewill Baptist sect, Benjamen Randel, was among Whitefield's last converts. Although originally much opposed to the "delusion and enthusiasm" of revivalism, he agreed to the persuasion of friends to hear Whitefield on September 25, 26, 1770, at the meeting house where Harvard's president, Samuel Langdon, worshipped. Whitefield died a week later, and Randel later converted after meditating on Whitefield's words and Hebrews 9:26.[19]

HARVARD'S POLARIZATION AGAINST THE NEW WAVE

Harvard at First Brushed by the Great Awakening

The Boston Gazette reported that "even Harvard" was "marvelously wrought upon" during the first visit of Whitefield in 1741.[20] The apparent stirring of godliness occurred in the context of Harvard's strict disciplinary system. From the founding of the College, for instance, stern discipline structured all of student life, enforceable even by corporal punishment. Later in May of 1755, Holyoke announced in chapel that thereafter corporal punishment could no longer be meted out. Contrary to decree, Holyoke broke a brand and birch rod in two, over the posterior of an accused. The Freshman's offense had been failure to commit to memory four thousand lines of Ovid for the 7:00 a.m. recitation the morning before.[21] Discipline even restricted free speech, disallowing criticism of College overseers:

18. Heimert and Miller, *The Great Awakening*, 506.

19. Marini, *Radical Sects of Revolutionary New England*, 64.

20. Gaustad, *The Great Awakening*, 30; Whitefield's *Seventh Journal*, 54-55.

21. Moe, *A History of Harvard*, 50.

THE SOCIOLOGICAL DIMENSION OF THEIR INTERRELATION

> [I]f any Scholar, Graduate or Undergraduate make Resistance to the President or any of the Professor or Tutors such Scholar shall be liable to Degradation or Expulsion. And it any Scholar offer Violence or any heinous insult to any of the Governors of the College, he shall be forthwith expelled.[22]

A committee appointed by the State in 1723 to investigate the affairs of the College returned the following vivid report:

> Although there is a considerable number of virtuous and studious youths in the college, yet there has been a practice of several immoralities, particularly stealing, lying, swearing, idleness, picking of locks, and the frequent use of strong drink ... that the scholars, many of them, are too long absent from the college ... that the scholars do generally spend too much of the Saturday evening in one another's chambers, and that the Freshmen, as well as others, are seen in great numbers going to town on Sabbath mornings to provide breakfasts.[23]

The year before strong liquor was allowed into the student's rooms.[24] "Things came to such a pass that the whole Colony began to fear for the good name of Harvard."[25]

On September 24th, 1741, Whitefield preached at the first church of Cambridge, where the president of the College, many tutors and students heard him preach on the text "we are not as men who corrupt the Word of God." Whitefield had been guided by more conservative clergy concerned with the direction of the college.[26] In his journal he represents himself as having been "treated and entertained very civilly by the President of the College." On another occasion, he chronicled, "Being at the College, I preached on the qualifications proper for a true evangelical preacher of

---

22. *The Body of Law for Harvard College* (1734 [handwritten Harvard archives]), chapter 8.14.
23. Moe, *A History of Harvard*, 46.
24. Ibid.
25. Ibid.
26. Quincy, 2:41.

Christ's righteousness. The Lord opened my mouth, and I spoke very plainly to tutors and pupils."[27] Whitefield concluded in his journal that Harvard College was "not far superior to the University of Oxford in piety and godliness."[28] Whitefield summarized his concern of the College's doctrinal and moral development:

> The chief College in New England, has one President, four Tutors, and about a hundred students. It is scarce as big as one of our least Colleges at Oxford, and, as far as I could gather from some, who well knew the state of it, not far superior to our Universities in piety and true godliness. Tutors neglect to pray with, and examine the hearts of, their pupils. Discipline is at too low an ebb. Bad books are become fashionable amongst them. Tillotson and Clarke are read instead of Shepard and Stoddard, and such like evangelical writers; and therefore I chose to preach on these words, 'We are not as many who corrupt the word of God.'[29]

Gilbert Tennent commented on the after effect of Whitefield's ministry upon the undergraduates:

> Many Scholars appeared to be in great concern as to their souls. They prayed together, sung Psalms, and discoursed together 2 or 3 at a time and read good books. They told eagerly of their visions, convictions, assurances, and consolations. One 'pretended to see the devil in shape of a bear coming to his bedside'; some were 'under great terrors'; other 'had a succession of clouds and Comforts'; some talked of 'the free grace of God in Election and of the decrees.' Tennent counseled one of the students that the Almighty's decrees were above them and they should not much trouble themselves about them at present.[30]

The *Boston Gazette*, however, reported in April and June of 1741 that the scholars of the College were "in general wonderfully

---

27. Quincy, 2: 40-54.
28. Quincy, 1: 392.
29. Quincy, 2:40-41; Whitefield's *Seventh Journal*, Edit. 1741, 28.
30. Morison, *Three Centuries of Harvard*, 86.

wrought upon"[31] before Whitefield's sermon on September 24, 1741. Whitefield's initial interaction with Harvard was not entirely a "honeymoon" syndrome. Wigglesworth of Harvard took Whitefield to task for the mistake to assume the origin of "dream and suggestion, and anything which bears strongly upon the mind, as from the spirit of God."[32]

In 1741 Colman wrote exuberantly to Whitefield about the revival continuing in full swing: "the Work of God with us goes on greatly ... our crowded serious Assemblies continue and great Additions are made to our Churches. Yesterday no less than nineteen ..." The next year Colman wrote Whitefield that even Harvard had been touched.[33] The Harvard archives include the following handwritten report describing the revival of religion on campus dated June 4, 1741:

> [T]he committees of the Overseers chosen to make inquiry into the state of the college now makes the following report—now having met this day in the library, I make enquiry into the state of the College, of the President, Fellows, Professors and Tutors, we find that of late extraordinary and happy impressions of a religious nature have been made on the minds of great numbers of the students, by which the College is in better order than usual, and exercises of the President and Tutors better attended.[34]

Whitefield's Judgment of Harvard in 1741

The day Whitefield left new England in October 1741, he recorded his reflections: "As for the Universities, I believe it maybe said, their Light is become Darkness, Darkness that may be felt, and is complained of by the most godly Ministers." Whitefield's experience in New England overall, however, was pleasant:

31. *Boston Gazette*, April 20th, 1741; June 29th, 1741.
32. Quincy, 1: 574-75.
33. *Proceedings of the MHS*, LIII, 197f.; Gaustad, *The Great Awakening*, 51.
34. Pierce, *A History of Harvard University*, 175.

THE INTERRELATION OF THE GREAT AWAKENING AND HARVARD

> In short, I like New England exceeding well; and when a Spirit of Reformation revives, it certainly will prevail more than in any other place, because they are similar in their Worship, less corrupt in their Principles, and consequently easier to be brought over to the Form of sound Words, into which so many of their pious Ancestors were delivered.

Interestingly, the Records of the Overseers of Harvard University do not contain an entry in regard to Whitefield's visit in September 1741.[35] On Whitefield's second visit to New England, however, he and fellow-exhorters at times denounced Harvard as a "house of impiety and sin."[36] According to Morison "there was just enough notion of academic freedom to give Harvard a bad name among strict Calvinists."[37] Although maintaining inspectorial vigilance, during the days of Holyoke, Congregationalism and Harvard College were broadening down from primitive Calvinism toward Unitarian Pelagianism.[38]

Charles Chauncy's Sermon against Enthusiasm One Week after Harvard's 1742 Commencement the Catalyst for Polarization

Ministers who did not support the revival were driven to the brink by the sermon of one David McGregore (1710-? d. unknown), pastor of a Presbyterian congregation in Londonderry, New Hampshire, delivered to the Brattle Street Church on November 3, 1741. McGregore identified the core of the revival as a doctrinal and intellectual cleanup of the muddy theology, generically called Arminianism, which blocked divine light from shining upon New England. Enemies of the revival were enemies of the faith once for

---

35. *Cf. Records of the Overseers of Harvard University*, Volume 1 (Dec. 4, 1707 to Oct. 4, 1743) [handwritten Harvard archives].
36. Morison, 87.
37. Morison, 83.
38. Morison, 84.

all delivered to the Puritan fathers—historic Calvinism. Enemies of the old paths were traducers of those of the old faith.[39]

In rebuttal, the Lord's Day after Harvard's commencement in 1742, Charles Chauncy, grandson and namesake of a Harvard president, left center, polarizing himself and his followers as flagrant opponents of the revival. Chauncy, conspicuously silent on any positive features of the revival, upbraided the then common phenomenon of flocking to hear what his colleague Thomas Foxcroft called "evangelic preaching." This sermon functioned as a catalyst polarizing New England into pro-revivalist and non-revivalist factions. Chauncy's prestige immediately propelled him to the height of the faction of all New Englanders who either ignored, feared, resented, or lambasted the revival.[40] Bacon quipped that "storms in the natural world are more apt to occur about the equinoxia, when the days and nights are equal; so when sects do grow to equality, there is apt to be more rivalry."[41] Both pro-revival and anti-revival, pro-Whitefield and anti-Whitefield, and orthodox and heterodox forces formed ideological battle lines. Whitefield himself, more than any other personage or doctrine, became the "Shibboleth" to distinguish in which "camp" one held residency.

Harvard's Denunciation of Whitefield in 1744

In April 1741, two consecutive issues of the Boston Gazette were comprised largely of a long letter written by William Brattle, rebuking Whitefield for hasty and unfounded judgments. In July Whitefield sought to ameliorate the ill feeling in a conciliatory letter, almost but not quite apologetic: "To the students, &c. under convictions at the colleges of Cambridge and New-Haven,—in New-England and Connecticut."[42]

---

39. David McGregore, "The Spirits of the Present Day Tried. A Sermon at the Tuesday Evening Lecture in Brattle Street, Boston" (Boston, 1742), 1-3, 11-25; Heimert and Miller, *The Great Awakening*, 214-15.
40. Heimert and Miller, *The Great Awakening*, 228-29.
41. Clarke, *Orthodox Congregationalism and the Sects*, 76.
42. Whitefield, "A Letter to the President," in Lovejoy, ed. *Religious*

Whitefield's announcement in 1744 of his intent to return to New England, however, further polarized—even mobilized—the opposing factions of the populace. Upon the announcement, parties favorable and unfavorable braced themselves for the new wave of religious fervor certain to attend his visit. The pinnacle of resistance to the soon return of the evangelist consisted of a testimonial drafted by Harvard President Edward Holyoke with the faculty. The testimonial is not against Edwards nor the revival per se; rather, the diatribe assails Whitefield himself.[43] Ill feeling only grew between 1741 and 1744, and by 1744 Harvard drafted a formal charge.[44] Yale followed with its own formal testimony the next year.[45]

Harvard College calcified in denunciation of Whitefield, entitling him an "enthusiast, a censorious, uncharitable person, and a deluder of the people."[46] Before the formal charge, President Holyoke, in an open letter, joined the chorus of critics, telling Whitefield that "the furious zeal with which you had so fired the passion of the people hath, in many places, burnt up the very vitals of religion; and a censorious, unpeaceable, uncharitable disposition hath, in multitudes, usurped the place of a godly jealousy."[47]

Harvard accused Whitefield of speaking like a man who believed he had direct communication from God and as much intimacy with him "as any of the Prophets and Apostles." Whitefield answered the Harvard community that he certainly had communion with God, "to a Degree," and had he not, he never would have become a minister. "In what other way are saints chosen?" he asked. "To Talk of ... having the Spirit of God without feeling it,

---

Enthusiasm, 106.

43. Heimert and Miller, *The Great Awakening*, 340-41.

44. *The Testimony of the President, Professors, Tutors and Hebrew Instructor of Harvard College in Cambridge, Against the Reverend Mr. George Whitefield, And his Conduct* (Boston, 1744).

45. *The Declaration of the Rector and Tutors of Yale-College in New-Haven, against the Reverend Mr. George Whitefield, his principles and designs. In a letter to him* (Boston, 1745).

46. Quincy, *History of Harvard*, 2, p. 56.

47. Quincy, 2, p. 57.

is really to deny the Thing." Whitefield claims no "false sprit" but declared his communion with God to be the real thing.[48]

The Testimony of 1744 is not innuendo, but rather an explication, from its first sentence, that Whitefield himself is a dangerous man. The Testimony charges him with groundless religious emotion, or enthusiasm, slander, fraud in the use of funds, and extemporaneous itinerant preaching. The charge of enthusiasm smacks of a disdain for intellectualism. The Harvard establishment, steeped in the love of reason,[49] looked down at those so under the sway of their emotions. The Testimony objects to the naming of ministers whom Whitefield believed to be unconverted, arguing that if Whitefield believed a minister was unconverted he should keep that to himself, not publish his conclusion in his journal. Further, donations ostensibly for an orphanage required an accounting, according to the Harvard establishment,[50] especially in that the orphanage had been left to the care of a Quaker. Not long before, Judge Samuel Sewall even voted against a building permit for the construction of a Quaker meeting house, calling their religion "devil worship." Moreover, extemporaneous preaching was dangerous because unguarded statements, even from the most articulate of preachers, were bound to slip out. The Testimony cites only two examples, however, the statements "God loves sinners as sinners" and "Christ loves unregenerate Sinners with a Love of Complacency." Last, the Harvard critics thought that pure itineracy was unbiblical, that is, possessing no normative example

---

48. "Testimony against George Whitefield," in Heimert and Miller, *Great Awakening*, 346; Whitefield, "A Letter to the President," in Lovejoy, ed., *Religious Enthusiasm*, 106.

49. Works of Nathaneal Tayler (d. 1702) demonstrated a concern against the trend of preferring reason over revelation. Conservatives tended to view rationalism as skepticism of divine revelation. Franklin Baumer, for instance, distinguishes skepticism from Calvin's *vera* or *legitima religio*, which is religion articulated by God in His Word. Baumer, *Religion and the Rise of Scepticism*, 27.

50. Donations were recorded, with the donors' names, in the archives of the College, which were accessible to the public. *Cf.* Benjamin Pierce, *Notes and Manuscripts for History* (Cambridge: [handwritten artifact, Harvard Archives]).

THE INTERRELATION OF THE GREAT AWAKENING AND HARVARD

in the New Testament. To be sure, ministers in New England preaching to other congregations was not uncommon (Edwards' "Sinners in the Hands of an Angry God" was preached the second time while he visited another congregation in Northhampton), but pure itineracy, a bird without a nest, was unbiblical in their view.[51]

The denunciation of Whitefield, however, was not a universal representation of the entire Harvard community. Josiah Smith, for instance, the first South Carolinian to be educated at Harvard, defended Whitefield tooth and nail, creed and character, both as a person and a preacher. Smith pastored the Independent Congregational Church in Charleston, South Carolina.[52]

Harvard Producing the Far-Left Wing of the Polarization against the Awakening

Harvard graduate Jonathan Mayhew (1720-66), although brushed at first by the Awakening's wings, reacted almost violently into a "rational religion" too extreme even for most all of the non-revivalists. He was viewed by his ministerial peers as brilliant as he was unorthodox. So much so that no Boston minister would participate in his ordination in 1747. In the 1750s he blurted outright denunciations of Chalcedonian Christianity, opting for at least a latent Unitarianism.[53] Indeed, Mayhew was a forerunner of more heterodoxy to come.[54] In the future context of nineteenth-century

---

51. The Testimony of the President, Professors, Tutors, and Hebrew Instructor of Harvard College, against George Whitefield (Boston, 1744).

52. Josiah Smith, "A Sermon, on the Character, Preaching, &c. of the Rev. Mr. Whitefield (1740)," in *George Whitefield, Fifteen Sermons Preached on Various Important Subjects* (New York, 1794), 16-21, 26-27, in Heimert and Miller, *The Great Awakening*, 62.

53. Heimert and Miller, *The Great Awakening*, 575.

54. Hollis Professor at Harvard Henry Ware published in 1820 in Cambridge *Letters to Trinitarians and Calvinists*, wherein he denied the doctrines of both. Foster, *A Genetic History of the New England Theology*, 307-08. In order to secure a sizable donation in 1879, for instance, Harvard Divinity School made clear that its curriculum no longer carried the heavy impress of Calvin, Edwards, Stuart, and Hodge like the orthodox seminaries. Williams,

developments, for instance, Mayhew's contribution was somewhat of a Pandora's box.[55]

CONCLUSION

Cultural and socioeconomic forces often order societies more than their ostensible religions. Miller, however, has focused on the sociological dynamics of Harvard's relation with the Great Awakening to the exclusion of the spiritual and theological developments that

---

The Harvard Divinity School, 147.

55. Nineteenth-century developments mark the loss of almost all the Awakening's distinctives. The frameworks within which the social sciences would develop first emerged under the prestigious umbrella of Harvard. After the Civil War, Harvard expanded its secular and humanistic studies, incorporating the emerging German concept of social science. Vidich and Lyman, *Worldly Rejections of Religion,* 53. On both sides of the Atlantic, sociologists attempted to reconstitute moral unity in the face of ever-increasing materialism and ever-increasing decay of traditional moral absolutes. The new secularists sought a substitute to the all-but-shattered Puritan covenant.

Francis Greenwood Peabody (1847-1936), first professor of social ethics at the Divinity School, for instance, taught an Arminian theology he had developed at the University of Halle as a basis for social reform (Vidich and Lyman, 53). In sum, Peabody argued that the solution to social problems involved a reaffirmation of Christian love and the injunction that each must lose their life in order to gain it. He outlined a model, a "social hero," an individual motivated not by self-interest prudence, or historical determinims but by "loyalty to an ideal." This loyalty would elevate society to a "realistic and rational line of melioristic conduct" (Vidich and Lyman, 65). Peabody's program was established as an independent department of social ethics in 1905, funded by philanthropist Alfred Tredway White, who donated more than $250,000 to endow both the Peabody program and Emerson Hall (Vidich and Lyman, 65). Peabody's brand of social ethics blossomed for a time in the melange of social science and problems courses from 1913 to 1920 (Vidich and Lyman, 65).

A student of Peabody, Edward Cummings (1861-1926), the first professor to teach sociology courses at Harvard, attempted to synthesize Christian-based socialism with the social psychology of Gustave Le Bon (1841) and Gabriel Tarde (1843-1904) (Vidich and Lyman, 53).

In general, Scottish moralists such as Spencer, English Fabians such as Beatrice and Sydney Wessb, German historicists such as Gustave von Schmoller, and economists such as David Ricardo and Karl Marx became spars for transatlantic adaptions, particularly to transmogrify the fundaments of Puritan theology into a secular social theory (Vidich and Lyman, 53-54).

motivated the opposing postures of the leaders of each faction. In the world view of the day, theology bore more of the New England mind than money. Christ was more of the focus of controversy than cultural/social class rivalry.

FINAL CONCLUSION

The fulcrum of divergent direction between Harvard and the Great Awakening, at least the Whitefieldian element, is neither cultural, social, economic, or legal. Theological differences propelled the factions into a collision course. At root, the way in which either "side" saw the Bible determined how they interpreted religious experience. Each side claimed to view the revival phenomenon through biblical eyeglasses, both claiming the "legitimacy" of being true heirs of the Puritan founders. Ultimately, exegetical differences determined doctrinal differences; and doctrinal opinions determined into which faction one would take one's stand.

Appendix A
MAYFLOWER COMPACT: 1620
Agreement between the Settlers at New Plymouth

IN THE NAME OF GOD, AMEN. We, whose names are underwritten, the Loyal Subjects of our dread Sovereign Lord King *James*, by the Grace of God, of *Great Britain, France,* and *Ireland,* King, *Defender of the Faith,* &c. Having undertaken for the Glory of God, and Advancement of the Christian Faith, and the Honour of our King and Country, a Voyage to plant the first Colony in the northern Parts of *Virginia*; Do by these Presents, solemnly and mutually, in the Presence of God and one another, covenant and combine ourselves together into a civil Body Politick, for our better Ordering and Preservation, and Furtherance of the Ends aforesaid: And by Virtue hereof do enact, constitute, and frame, such just and equal Laws, Ordinances, Acts, Constitutions, and Officers, from time to time, as shall be thought most meet and convenient for the general Good of the Colony; unto which we promise all due Submission and Obedience. **IN WITNESS** whereof we have hereunto subscribed our names at *Cape-Cod* the eleventh of November, in the Reign of our Sovereign Lord King *James,* of *England, France,* and *Ireland,* the eighteenth, and of *Scotland* the fifty-fourth, *Anno Domini*; 1620.

Mr. John Carver,	Mr Edward Winslow,
Mr. William Bradford,	Mr. William Brewster.

APPENDIX A

Isaac Allerton,
Myles Standish,
John Alden,
John Turner,
Francis Eaton,
James Chilton,
John Craxton,
John Billington,
Joses Fletcher,
John Goodman,
Mr. Samuel Fuller,
Mr. Christopher Martin,
Mr. William Mullins,
Mr. William White,
Mr. Richard Warren,
John Howland,
Mr. Steven Hopkins,
Digery Priest,
Thomas Williams,

Gilbert Winslow,
Edmund Margesson,
Peter Brown,
Richard Britteridge
George Soule,
Edward Tilly,
John Tilly,
Francis Cooke,
Thomas Rogers,
Thomas Tinker,
John Ridgdale
Edward Fuller,
Richard Clark,
Richard Gardiner,
Mr. John Allerton,
Thomas English,
Edward Doten,
Edward Liester.

Source: Yale Law School The Avalon Project https://avalon.law.yale.edu/17th_century/mayflower.asp

Appendix B
THE CHARTER OF MASSACHUSETTS BAY: 1629

CHARLES, BY THE, GRACE, OF GOD, Kinge of England, Scotland, Fraunce, and Ireland, Defendor of the Fayth, &c. To all to whome theis Presents shall come Greeting. WHEREAS, our most Deare and Royall Father, Kinge James, of blessed Memory, by his Highnes Letters-patents bearing Date at Westminster the third Day of November, in the eighteenth Yeare of His Raigne, HATH given and graunted vnto the Councell established at Plymouth, in the County of Devon, for the planting, ruling, ordering, and governing of Newe England in America, and to their Successors and Assignes for ever all that Parte of America, lyeing and being in Bredth, from Forty Degrees of Northerly Latitude from the Equinoctiall Lyne, to forty eight Degrees Of the saide Northerly Latitude inclusively, and in Length, of and within all the Breadth aforesaid, throughout the Maine Landes from Sea to Sea; together also with all the Firme Landes, Soyles, Groundes, Havens, Portes, Rivers, Waters, Fishing, Mynes, and Myneralls, as well Royall Mynes of Gould and Silver, as other Mynes ind Mvneralls, precious Stones, Quarries, and all and singular other Comodities, Jurisdiccons, Royalties, Priviledges, Franchesies, and Prehemynences, both within the said Tract of Land vpon the Mayne, and also within the Islandes and Seas adjoining: PROVIDED always, That the saide Islandes, or any the Premisses by the said Letters-patents intended and meant to be graunted, were not then actuallie possessed or inhabited, by any other Christian Prince or State, nor within the Boundes, Lymitts, or Territories of the Southerne Colony, then before graunted by our saide Deare Father, to be planted by divers of his loveing Subjects in the South Partes. TO HAVE and to houlde, possess, and enjoy all and singular the aforesaid Continent, Landes Territories, Islandes, Hereditaments, and Precincts, Seas, Waters, Fishings, with all, and all manner their Comodities, Royalties, Liberties, Prehemynences, and Proffits that should from thenceforth arise from thence, with all and singuler their Appurtenances, and every Parte and Parcell thereof, vnto the saide Councell and their Successors and Assignes for ever, to the sole and proper Vse, Benefitt, and Behoofe of them the saide Councell, and their Successors and Asignes for ever: To be houlden of our saide most Deare and Royall Father, his Heires and Successors, as of his Mannor of East Greenewich in the County of Kent, in free and comon Soccage, and not in Capite nor by Knight's Service: YEILDINGE and paying therefore to the saide late Kinge, his heires and Successors, the fifte Parte of the Oare of Gould and Silver, which should from tyme to tyme, and at all Tymes then after happen to be found, gotten, had, and obteyned in, att, or within any of the saide Landes, Lymitts, Territories, and Precincts, or in or within any Parte or Parcell thereof, for or in Respect of all and all Manner of Duties, Demaunds and Services whatsoever, to be don, made, or paide to our saide Dear Father the late Kinge his Heires and Successors, as in and by the saide Letters-patents (amongst sundrie and other Clauses, Powers, Priviledges, and Grauntes therein conteyned), more at large appeareth:

AND WHEREAS, the saide Councell established at Plymouth, in the County of Devon, for the plantinge, ruling, ordering, and governing of Newe England in America, have by their Deede, indented vnder their Comon Seale, bearing Date the nyneteenth Day of March last past, in the third Yeare of our Raigne, given, graunted, bargained, soulde, enfeofled, aliened, and confirmed to Sir Henry Rosewell, Sir John Young, Knightes, Thomas Southcott, John Humphrey, John Endecott, and Symon Whetcombe, their Heires and Assignes, and their Associats for ever, all that Parte

THE CHARTER OF MASSACHUSETTS BAY: 1629

of Newe England in America aforesaid, which lyes and extendes betweene a greate River there comonlie called Monomack alias Merriemack, and a certen other River there, called Charles River, being in the Bottome of a certayne Bay there, comonlie called Massachusetts, alias Mattachusetts, alias Massatusetts Bay, and also all and singuler those Landes and Hereditaments whatsoever, lyeing within the Space of three English Myles on the South Parte of the said Charles River, or of any, or everie Parte thereof; and also, all and singuler the Landes and Hereditaments whatsoever, lyeing and being within the Space of three English Myles to the Southward of the Southermost Parte of the saide Bay called Massachusetts, alias Mattachusetts, alias Massatusets Bay; and also, all those Landes and Hereditaments whatsoever, which lye, and be within the space of three English Myles to the Northward of the said River called Monomack, alias Merrymack, or to the Northward of any and every Parte thereof, and all Landes and Hereditaments whatsoever, lyeing within the Lymitts aforesaide, North and South in Latitude and breath, and in Length and Longitude, of and within all the Bredth aforesaide, throughout the Mayne Landes there, from the Atlantick and Westerne Sea and Ocean on the East Parte, to the South Sea on the West Parte; and all Landes and Groundes, Place and Places, Soyles, Woodes and Wood Groundes, Havens, Portes, Rivers, Waters, Fishings, and Hereditaments whatsoever, lyeing within the said Boundes and Lymitts, and everie Parte and Parcell thereof; and also, all Islandes lyeing in America aforesaid, in the saide Seas or either of them on the Westerne or Eastern Coastes or Partes of the said Tractes of Lande, by the saide Indenture mencoed to be given, graunted, bargained, sould, enfeofled, aliened, and confirmed, or any of them; and also, all Mynes and Myneralls, as well Royall Mynes of Gould and Silver, as other Mynes and Myneralls whatsoeuer, in the saide Lands and Premisses, or any Parte thereof; and all Jurisdiccons, Rights, Royalties, Liberties, Freedomes, Ymmunities, Priviledges, Franchises, Preheminences, and Comodities whatsoever, which they, the said Councell established at Plymouth, in the County of Devon, for the planting, ruling, ordering, and governing of Newe England in

America, then had, or might vse, exercise, or enjoy, in or within the saide Landes and Premisses by the saide Indenture mencoed to be given, graunted, bargained, sould, enfeoffed, and confirmed, or in or within any Parte or Parcell thereof:

To HAVE and to hould, the saide Parte of Newe England in America, which lyes and extendes and is abutted as aforesaide, and every Parte and Parcell thereof; and all the saide Islandes, Rivers, Portes, Havens, Waters, Fishings, Mynes, and Myneralls, Jurisdiccons, Franchises, Royalties, Liberties, Priviledges, Comodities, Hereditaments, and Premisses whatsoever, with the Appurtenances vnto the saide Sir Henry Rosewell, Sir John Younge, Thomas Southcott, John Humfrey, John Endecott, and Simon Whetcombe, their Heires and Assignes, and their Associatts, to the onlie proper and absolute vse and Behoofe of the said Sir Henry Rosewell, Sir John Younge, Thomas Southcott, John Humfrey, John Endecott, and Simon Whettcombe, their Heires and Assignes, and their Associatts forevermore; TO BE HOULDEN of Vs. our Heires and Successors, as of our Mannor of Eastgreenwich, in the County of Kent, in free and comon Soccage, and not in Capite, nor by Knightes Service; YEILDING and payeing therefore vnto Vs. our Heires and Successors, the fifte Parte of the Oare of Goulde and Silver, which shall from Tyme to Tyme, and at all Tymes hereafter, happen to be founde, gotten, had, and obteyned in any of the saide Landes, within the saide Lymitts, or in or witllin any Parte thereof, for, and in Satisfaccon of all manner Duties, Demaundes, and Services whatsoever to be done, made, or paid to Vs. our Heires or Successors, as in and by the said recited Indenture more at large maie appeare.

NOWE Knowe Yee, that Wee, at the humble Suite and Peticon of the saide Sir Henry Rosewell, Sir John Younge, Thomas Southcott, John Humfrey, John Endecott, and Simon Whetcombe, and of others whome they have associated vnto them, HAVE, for divers good Causes and consideracons, vs moveing, graunted and confirmed, and by theis Presents of our especiall Grace, certen Knowledge, and meere mocon, doe graunt and confirme vnto the

THE CHARTER OF MASSACHUSETTS BAY: 1629

saide Sir Henry Rosewell, Sir John Younge, Thomas Southcott, John Humfrey, John Endecott, and Simon Whetcombe, and to their Associatts hereafter named; (videlicet) Sir Richard Saltonstall, Knight, Isaack Johnson, Samuel Aldersey, John Ven, Mathew Cradock, George Harwood, Increase Nowell, Richard Perry, Richard Bellingham, Nathaniell Wright, Samuel Vassall, Theophilus Eaton, Thomas Goffe, Thomas Adams, John Browne, Samuell Browne, Thomas Hutchins, William Vassall, William Pinchion, and George Foxcrofte, their Heires and Assignes, all the saide Parte of Newe England in America, lyeing and extending betweene the Boundes and Lvmytts in the said recited Indenture expressed, and all Landes and Groundes, Place and Places, Soyles, Woods and Wood Groundes, Havens, Portes, Rivers, Waters, Mynes, Mineralls, Jurisdiccons, Rightes, Royalties, Liberties, Freedomes, Immunities, Priviledges, Franchises, Preheminences, Hereditaments, and Comodities whatsoever, to them the saide Sir Henry Rosewell, Sir John Younge, Thomas Southcott, John Humfrey, John Endecott, and Simon Whetcombe, theire Heires and Assignes, and to their Associatts, by the saide recited Indenture, given, graunted, bargayned, solde, enfeoffed, aliened, and confirmed, or mencoed or intended thereby to be given, graunted, bargayned, sold, enfeoffed, aliened, and confirmed: To HAVE, and to hould, the saide Parte of Newe England in America, and other the Premisses hereby mencoed to be graunted and confirmed, and every Parte and Parcell thereof with the Appurtenuces, to the saide Sir Henry Rosewell, Sir John Younge, Sir Richard Saltonstall, Thomas Southcott, John Humfrey, John Endecott, Simon Whetcombe, Isaack Johnson, Richard Pery, Richard Bellingham, Nathaniell Wright, Samuell Vassall, Theophilus Eaton, Thomas Gode, Thomas Adams, John Browne, Samuel Bromine, Thomas Hutchins, Samuel Aldersey, John Ven, Mathewe Cradock, George Harwood, Increase Nowell, William Vassall, William Pinchion, and George Foxcrofte, their Heires and Assignes forever, to their onlie proper and absolute Vse and Behoofe for evermore; To be holden of Vs. our Heires and Successors, as of our Mannor of Eastgreenewich aforesaid, in free and comon Socage, and not in Capite, nor by Knights Service;

APPENDIX B

AND ALSO YEILDING and paying therefore to Vs. our Heires and Successors, the fifte parte onlie of all Oare of Gould and Silver, which from tyme to tyme, and aft all tymes hereafter shalbe there gotten, had, or obteyned for all Services, Exaccons and Demaundes whatsoever, according to the Tenure and Reservacon in the said recited Indenture expressed.

AND FURTHER, knowe yee, that of our more especiall Grace, certen Knowledg, and meere mocon, Wee have given and graunted, and by theis Presents, doe for Vs. our Heires and Successors, give and graunte onto the saide Sir Henry Rosewell, Sir John Younge. Sir Richard Saltonstall, Thomas Southcott, John Humfrey, John Endecott, Symon Whetcombe, Isaack Johnson, Samuell Aldersey, John Ven, Mathewe Cradock, George Harwood, Increase Nowell, Richard Pery, Richard Bellingham, Nathaniel Wright, Samuell Vassall, Theophilus Eaton, Thomas Gode, Thomas Adams, John Browne, Samuell Browne, Thomas Hutchins, William Vassall, William Pinchion, and George Foxcrofte, their Heires and Assignes, all that Parte of Newe England in America, which lyes and extendes betweene a great River there, comonlie called Monomack River, alias Merrimack River, and a certen other River there, called Charles River, being in the Bottome of a certen Bay there, comonlie called Massachusetts, alias Mattachusetts, alias Massatusetts Bay; and also all and singuler those Landes and Hereditaments whatsoever, lying within the Space of Three Englishe Myles on the South Parte of the said River, called Charles River, or of any or every Parte thereof; and also all and singuler the Landes and Hereditaments whatsoever, lying and being within the Space of Three Englishe Miles to the southward of the southermost Parte of the said Baye, called Massachusetts, alias Mattachusetts, alias Massatusets Bay: And also all those Landes and Hereditaments whatsoever, which lye and be within the Space of Three English Myles to the Northward of the saide River, called Monomack, alias Merrymack, or to the Norward of any and every Parte thereof, and all Landes and Hereditaments whatsoever, lyeing within the Lymitts aforesaide, North and South, in Latitude and Bredth, and in Length and Longitude, of and within all the Bredth aforesaide, throughout the mayne Landes there, from the Atlantick and Westerne Sea and Ocean on the East Parte, to the South Sea on the West Parte; and all Landes and Groundes, Place and Places, Soyles, Woodes, and Wood Groundes, Havens, Portes, Rivers, Waters, and Hereditaments whatsoever, lyeing within the said Boundes and Lymytts, and every Parte and Parcell thereof; and also all Islandes in America aforesaide, in the saide Seas, or either of them, on the Westerne or Easterne Coastes, or Partes of the saide Tracts of Landes hereby mencoed to be given and graunted, or any of them; and all Mynes and Mynerals as well Royal mynes of Gold and Silver and other mynes and mynerals, whatsoever, in the said Landes and Premisses, or any parte thereof, and free Libertie of fishing in or within any the Rivers or Waters within the Boundes and Lymytts aforesaid, and the Seas therevnto adjoining; and all Fishes, Royal Fishes, Whales, Balan, Sturgions, and other Fishes of what Kinde or Nature soever, that shall at any time hereafter be taken in or within the saide Seas or Waters, or any of them, by the said Sir Henry Rosewell, Sir John Younge, Sir Richard Saltonstall, Thomas Southcott, John Humfrey, John Endecott, Simon Whetcombe, Isaack Johnson, Samuell Aldersey, John Ven, Mathewe Cradock, Greorge Harwood, Increase Noell, Richard Pery, Richard Bellingham, Nathaniell Wright, Samuell Vassell, Theophilus Eaton, Thomas Goffe, Thomas Adams, John Browne, Samuell Browner, Thomas Hutchins, William Vassall, William Pinchion, and George Foxcrofte, their Heires and Assignes, or by any other person or persons whatsoever there inhabiting, by them, or any of them, to be appointed to fishe therein.

 PROVIDED alwayes, That yf the said Landes, Islandes, or any other the Prernisses herein before menconed, and by theis presents, intended and meant to be graunted, were at the tyme of the graunting of the saide former Letters patents, dated the Third Day of November, in the Eighteenth Yeare of our said deare Fathers Raigne aforesaide, actuallie possessed or inhabited by any other Christian Prince or State, or were within the Boundes, Lymytts or Territories of that Southerne Colony, then before graunted by our said late Father, to be planted by divers of his loveing Subiects in the

APPENDIX B

south partes of America, That then this present Graunt shall not extend to any such partes or parcells thereof, soe formerly inhabited, or lyeing within the Boundes of the Southerne Plantacon as aforesaide, but as to those partes or parcells soe possessed or inhabited by such Christian Prince or State, or being within the Bounders aforesaide shal be vtterlie voyd, theis presents or any Thinge therein conteyned to the contrarie notwithstanding. To HAVE and hould, possesse and enioye the saide partes of New England in America, which lye, extend, and are abutted as aforesaide, and every parse and parcell thereof; and all the Islandes, Rivers, Portes, Havens, Waters, Fishings, Fishes, Mynes, Myneralls, Jurisdiccons, Franchises, Royalties, Liberties, Priviledges, Comodities, and Premisses whatsoever, with the Appurtenances, vnto the said Sir Henry Rosewell, Sir John Younge, Sir Richard Saltonstall, Thomas Southcott, John Humfrey, John Endecott, Simon Whetcombe, Isaack Johnson, Samuell Aldersey, John Yen, Mathewe Cradock, George Harwood, Increase Noweil, Richard Perry, Richard Bellingham, Nathaniell Wright, Samuell Vassall, Theophilus Eaton, Thomas Gofle, Thomas Adams, John Browne, Samuell Browne, Thomas Hutchins, William Vassall, William Pinchion, and George Foxeroft, their Heires and Assignes forever, to the onlie proper and absolute Vse and Behoufe of the said Sir Henry Rosewell, Sir John Younge, Sir Richard Saltonstall, Thomas Southcott, John Humfrey, John Endecott, Simon Whetcombe, Isaac Johnson, Samuell Aldersey, John Ven, Mathewe Cradocke, George Harwood, Increase Noweil, Richard Pery, Richard Bellingham, Nathaniell Wright, Samuell Vassall, Theophilus Eaton, Thomas Goffe, Thomas Adams, John Browne, Samuell Browne, Thomas Hutchins, William Vassall, William Pinchion, and George Foxcroft, their Heires and Assignes forevermore: To BE HOLDEN of Vs. our Heires and Successors, as of our Manor of Eastgreenwich in our Countie of Kent, within our Realme of England, in free and comon Soccage, and not in Capite, nor by Knights Service; and also yeilding and paying therefore, to Vs. our Heires and Sucessors, the fifte Parte onlie of all Oare of Gould and Silver, which from tyme to tyme, and at all tymes hereafter, shal be there gotten, had, or obteyned, for all Services,

THE CHARTER OF MASSACHUSETTS BAY: 1629

Exaccons, and Demaundes whatsoever; PROVIDED alwaies, and our expresse Will and Meaninge is, that onlie one fifte Parte of the Gould and Silver Oare above mencoed, in the whole, and noe more be reserved or payeable vnto Vs. our Heires and Successors, by Collour or Vertue of theis Presents, the double Reservacons or rentals aforesaid or any Thing herein conteyned notwithstanding. AND FORASMUCH, as the good and prosperous Successe of the Plantacon of the saide Partes of Newe-England aforesaide intended by the said Sir Henry Rosewell, Sir John Younge, Sir Richard Saltonstall, Thomas Southcott, John Humfrey, John Endecott, Simon Whetcombe, Isaack Johnson, Samuell Aldersey John Ven, Mathew Cradock, George Harwood, Increase Noell, Richard Pery, Richard Bellingham, Nathaniell Wright, Samuell Vassall, Theophilus Eaton, Thomas Goffe, Thomas Adams, John Browne, Samuell Browne, Thomas Hutchins, William Vassall, William Pinchion, and George Foxcrofte, to be speedily sett vpon, cannot but cheifly depend, next vnder the Blessing of Almightie God, and the support of our Royall Authoritie vpon the good Government of the same, To the Ende that the Affaires and Buyssinesses which from tyme to tyme shall happen and arise concerning the saide Landes, and the Plantation of the same maie be the better mannaged and ordered, WEE HAVE FURTHER hereby of our especial Grace, certain Knowledge and mere Mocon, Given, graunted and confirmed, and for Vs. our Heires and Successors, doe give, graunt, and confirme vnto our said trustie and welbeloved subjects Sir Henry Rosewell, Sir John Younge, Sir Richard Saltonstall, Thomas Southcott, John Humfrey, John Endicott, Simon Whetcombe, Isaack Johnson, Samuell Aldersey, John Yen, Mathewe Cradock, George Harwood, Increase Nowell, Richard Pery, Richard Bellingham, Nathaniell Wright, Samuell Vassall, Theophilus Eaton, Thomas Goffe, Thomas Adams, John Browne, Samuell Browne, Thomas Hutchins, William Vassall, William Pinchion, and George Foxcrofte: AND for Vs. our Heires and Successors, Wee will and ordeyne, That the saide Sir Henry Rosewell, Sir John Young, Sir Richard Saltonstall, Thomas Southcott, John Humfrey, John Endicott, Svmon Whetcombe, Isaack Johnson, Samuell Aldersey,

APPENDIX B

John Ven, Mathewe Cradock, George Harwood, Increase Noell, Richard Pery, Richard Bellingham, Nathaniell Wright, Samuell Vassall, Theophilus Eaton, Thomas Goffe, Thomas Adams, John Browne, Samuell Browne, Thomas Hutchins, William Vassall, William Pinchion, and George Foxcrofte, and all such others as shall hereafter be admitted and made free of the Company and Society hereafter mencoed, shall from tyme to tyme, and att all tymes forever hereafter be, by Vertue of theis presents, one Body corporate and politique in Fact and Name, by the Name of the Governor and Company of the Mattachusetts Bay in Newe-England, and them by the Name of the Governour and Company of the Mattachusetts Bay in Newe-England, one Bodie politique and corporate, in Deede, Fact, and Name; Wee doe for vs. our Heires and Successors, make, ordoyne, constitute, and confirme by theis Presents, and that by that name they shall have perpetuall Succession, and that by the same Name they and their Successors shall and maie be capeable and enabled aswell to implead, and to be impleaded, and to prosecute, demaund, and aunswere, and be aunsweared veto, in all and singuler Suites, Causes, Quarrells, and Accons, of what kinde or nature soever. And also to have, take, possesse, acquire, and purchase any Landes, Tenements, or Hereditaments, or any Goodes or Chattells, and the same to lease, graunte, demise, alien, bargaine, sell, and dispose of, as other our liege People of this our Realme of England, or any other corporacon or Body politique of the same may lawfully doe.

AND FURTHER, That the said Governour and Companye, and their Successors, maie have forever one comon Seale, to be vsed in all Causes and Occasions of the said Company, and the same Seale may alter, chaunge, breake, and newe make, from tyme to tyme, at their pleasures. And our Will and Pleasure is, and Wee doe hereby for Vs. our Heires and Successors, ordeyne and graunte, That from henceforth for ever, there shalbe one Governor, one Deputy Governor, and eighteene Assistants of the same Company, to be from tyme to tyme constituted, elected and chosen out of the Freemen of the saide Company, for the tyme being, in such Manner and Forme as hereafter in theis Presents is expressed, which said Officers shall applie themselves to take Care for the best disposeing and ordering of the generall buysines and Affaires of, for, and concerning the said Landes and Premisses hereby mencoed, to be graunted, and the Plantacion thereof, and the Government of the People there. AND FOR the better Execucon of our Royall Pleasure and Graunte in this Behalf, WEE doe, by theis presents, for Vs. our Heires and Successors, nominate, ordeyne, make, & constitute; our welbeloved the saide Mathewe Cradocke, to be the first and present Governor of the said Company, and the saide Thomas Goffe, to be Deputy Governor of the saide Company, and the saide Sir Richard Saltonstall, Isaack Johnson, Samuell Aldersey, John Ven, John Humfrey, John Endecott, Simon Whetcombe, Increase Nowell, Richard Pery, Nathaniell Wright, Samuell Vassall, Theophilus Eaton, Thomas Adams, Thomas Hutchins, John Browne, George Foxcrofte, William Vassall, and William Pinchion, to be the present Assistants of the saide Company, to continue in the saide several Offices respectivelie for such tyme, and in such manner, as in and by theis Presents is hereafter declared and appointed.

AND FURTHER, Wee will, and by theis Presents, for Vs. our Heires and Successors, doe ordoyne and graunte, That the Governor of the saide Company for the tyme being, or in his Absence by Occasion of Sicknes or otherwise, the Deputie Governor for the tyme being, shall have Authoritie from tyme to tyme vpon all Occasions, to give order for the assembling of the saide Company, and calling them together to consult and advise of the Bussinesses and Affaires of the saide Company, and that the said Governor, Deputie Governor, and Assistants of the saide Company, for the tyme being, shall or maie once every Moneth, or oftener at their Pleasures, assemble and houlde and keepe a Courte or Assemblie of themselves, for the better ordering and directing of their Affaires, and that any seaven or more persons of the Assistants, togither with the Governor, or Deputie Governor soe assembled, shalbe saide, taken, held, and reputed to be, and shalbe a full and sufficient Courte or Assemblie of the said Company, for the handling, ordering, and dispatching of all such Buysinesses and Occurrents

APPENDIX B

as shall from tyme to tyme happen, touching or concerning the said Company or Plantacon; and that there shall or maie be held and kept by the Governor, or Deputie Governor of the said Company, and seaven or more of the said Assistants for the tyme being, vpon every last Wednesday in Hillary, Easter, Trinity, and Michas Termes respectivelie forever, one grease generall and solempe assemblie, which foure generall assemblies shalbe stiled and called the foure grease and generall Courts of the saide Company; IN all and every, or any of which saide grease and generall Courts soe assembled, WEE DOE for Vs. our Heires and Successors, give and graunte to the said Governor and Company, and their Successors, That the Governor, or in his absence, the Deputie Governor of the saide Company for the tyme being, and such of the Assistants and Freeman of the saide Company as shalbe present, or the greater nomber of them so assembled, whereof the Governor or Deputie Governor and six of the Assistants at the least to be seaven shall have full Power and authoritie to choose, nominate, and appointe, such and soe many others as they shall thinke fitt, and that shall be willing to accept the same, to be free of the said Company and Body, and them into the same to admits; and to elect and constitute such Officers as they shall thinke fitt and requisite, for the ordering, mannaging, and dispatching of the Affaires of the saide Govenor and Company, and their Successors; And to make Lawes and Ordinnces for the Good and Welfare of the saide Company, and for the Government and ordering of the saide Landes and Plantacon, and the People inhabiting and to inhabite the same, as to them from tyme to tyme shalbe thought meete, soe as such Lawes and Ordinances be not contrarie or repugnant to the Lawes and Statuts of this our Reaime of England. AND, our Will and Pleasure is, and Wee doe hereby for Vs, our Heires and Successors, establish and ordeyne, That yearely once in the yeare, for ever hereafter, namely, the last Wednesdav in Easter Tearme, yearely, the Governor, Deputy-Governor, and Assistants of the saide Company and all other officers of the saide Company shalbe in the Generall Court or Assembly to be held for that Day or Tyme, newly chosen for the Yeare ensueing by such greater parse of the said Company, for the Tyme being, then and there present, as is aforesaide. AND, yf it shall happen the present governor, Deputy Governor, and assistants, by theis presents appointed, or such as shall hereafter be newly chosen into their Roomes, or any of them, or any other of the officers to be appointed for the said Companv, to dye, or to be removed from his or their severall Offices or Places before the saide generall Day of Eleccon (whome Wee doe hereby declare for any Misdemeanor or Defect to be removeable by the Governor, Deputie Governor, Assistants, and Company, or such greater Parte of them in any of the publique Courts to be assembled as is aforesaid) That then, and in every such Case, it shall and maie be lawfull, to and for the Governor, Deputie Governor, Assistants, and Company aforesaide, or such greater Parte of them soe to be assembled as is aforesaide, in any of their Assemblies, to proceade to a new Eleccon of one or more others of their Company in the Roome or Place, Roomes or Places of such Officer or Officers soe dyeing or removed according to their Discrecons, And, Mediately vpon and after such Eleccon and Eleccons made of such Governor, Deputie Governor, Assistant or Assistants, or any other officer of the saide Company, in Manner and Forme aforesaid, the Authoritie, Office, and Power, before given to the former Governor, Deputie Governor, or other Officer and Officers soe removed, in whose Steade and Place newe shabe soe chosen, shall as to him and them, and everie of them, cease and determine

PROVIDED alsoe, and our Will and Pleasure is, That aswell such as are by theis Presents appointed to be the present Governor, Deputie Governor, and Assistants of the said Company, as those that shall Succeed them, and all other Officers to be appointed and chosen as aforesaid, shall, before they undertake the Execucon of their saide Offices and Places respectivelie, take their Corporal Oathes for the due and faithfull Performance of their Duties in their severall Offices and Places, before such Person or Persons as are by theis Presents hereunder appointed to take and receive the same; That is to saie, the saide Mathewe Cradock, whoe is hereby nominated and appointed the present Governor of the saide Company, shall take the saide Oathes before one or more of the Masters

APPENDIX B

of our Courte of Chauncery for the Tyme being, vnto which Master or Masters of the Chauncery, Wee doe by theis Presents give full Power and Authoritie to take and administer the said Oathe to the said Governor accordinglie: And after the saide Governor shalbe soe sworne, then the said Deputy Governor and Assistants, before by theis Presents nominated and appointed, shall take the said severall Oathes to their Offices and Places respectivelie belonging, before the said Mathew Cradock, the present Governor, soe formerlie sworne as aforesaide. And every such person as shall be at the Tyme of the annuall Eleccon, or otherwise, vpon Death or Removeall, be appointed to be the newe Governor of the said Company, shall take the Oathes to that Place belonging, before the Deputy Governor, or two of the Assistants of the said Company at the least, for the Tyme being: And the newe elected Deputie Governor and Assistants, and all other officers to be hereafter chosen as aforesaide from Tyme to Tyme, to take the Oathes to their places respectivelie belonging, before the Governor of the said Company for the Tyme being, vnto which said Governor, Deputie Governor, and assistants, Wee doe by theis Presents Give full Power and Authoritie to give and administer the said Oathes respectively, according to our true Meaning herein before declared, without any Comission or further Warrant to be had and obteyned of our Vs. our Heires or Successors, in that Behalf. AND, Wee doe further, of our especial Grace, certen Knowledge, and meere mocon, for Vs. our Heires and Successors, give and graunte to the said Governor and Company, and their Successors for ever by theis Presents, That it shalbe lawfull and free for them and their Assignes, at all and every Tyme and Tymes hereafter, out of any our Realmes or Domynions whatsoever, to take, leade, carry, and transport, for in and into their Voyages, and for and towardes the said Plantacon in Newe England, all such and soe many of our loving Subjects, or any other strangers that will become our loving Subjects, and live under our Allegiance, as shall willinglie accompany them in the same Voyages and Plantacon; and also Shippmg, Armour, Weapons, Ordinance, Municon, Powder, Shott, Come, Victualls, and all Manner of clothing, Implements, Furniture, Beastes, Cattle,

Horses, Mares, Merchandizes, and all other Thinges necessarie for the saide Plantacon, and for their Vse and Defence, and for Trade with the People there, and in passing and returning to and fro, any Lawe or Statute to the contrarie hereof in any wise notwithstanding; and without payeing or yeilding any Custome or Subsidie, either inward or outward, to Vs. our Heires or Successors, for the same, by the Space of seaven Yeares from the Day of the Date of theis Presents. PROVIDED, that none of the saide Persons be such as shalbe hereafter by especiall Name restrayned by Vs. our Heires or Successors. AND, for their further Encouragement, of our especiall Grace and Favor, Wee doe by theis Presents, for Vs. our Heires and Successors, yeild and graunt to the saide Governor and Company, and their Successors, and every of them, their Factors and Assignes, That they and every of them shalbe free and quits from all Taxes, Subsidies, and Customes, in Newe England, for the like Space of seaven Yeares, and from all Taxes and Imposicons for the Space of twenty and one Yeares, vpon all Goodes and Merchandizes at any Tyme or Tymes hereafter, either vpon Importacon thither, or Exportacon from thence into our Realme of England, or into any other our Domynions by the said Governor and Company, and their Successors, their Deputies, Factors, and Assignes, or any of them; EXCEPT onlie the five Pounds per Centum due for Custome vpon all such Goodes and Merchandizes as after the saide seaven Yeares shalbe expired, shalbe brought or imported into our Realme of England, or any other of our Dominions, according to the aunciente Trade of Merchants, which five Poundes per Centum onlie being paide, it shall be thenceforth lawfull and free for the said Adventurers, the same Goodes and Merchandizes to export and carry out of our said Domynions into forraine Partes, without any Custome, Tax or other Dutie to be paid to Vs. our Heires or Successors, or to any other Officers or Ministers of Vs. our Heires and Successors. PROVIDED, that the said Goodes and Merchandizes be shipped out within thirteene Monethes, after their first Landing within any Parte of the saide Domynions.

AND, Wee doe for Vs. our Heires and Successors, give and graunte vnto the saide Governor and Company, and their

Successors, That whensoever, or soe often as any Custome or Subsedie shall growe due or payeable vnto Vs our Heires, or Successors, according to the Lymittacon and Appointment aforesaide, by Reason of any Goodes, Wares, or Merchandizes to be shipped out, or any Retorne to be made of any Goodes, Wares, or Merchandize vnto or from the said Partes of Newe England hereby moncoed to be graunted as aforesaid, or any the Landes or Territories aforesaide, That then, and soe often, and in such Case, the Farmors, Customers, and Officers of our Customes of England and Ireland, and everie of them for the Tyme being, vpon Request made to them by the saide Governor and Company, or their Successors, Factors or Assignes, and vpon convenient Security to be given in that Behalf, shall give and allowe vnto the said Governor and Company, and their Successors, and to all and everie Person and Persons free of that Company, as aforesaide, six Monethes Tyme for the Payement of the one halfe of all such Custome and Subsidy as shalbe due and payeable unto Vs. our Heires and Successors, for the same; for which theis our Letters patent, or the Duplicate, or the inrollemt thereof, shalbe vnto our saide Officers a sufficient Warrant and Discharge. NEVERTHELESS, our Will and Pleasure is, That yf any of the saide Goodes, Wares, and Merchandize, which be, or shalbe at any Tyme hereafter landed or exported out of any of our Realmes aforesaide, and shalbe shipped with a Purpose not to be carried to the Partes of Newe England aforesaide, but to some other place, That then such Payment, Dutie, Custome, Imposicon, or Forfeyfure, shalbe paid, or belonge to Vs. our Heires and Successors, for the said Goodes, Wares, and Merchandize, soe fraudulently sought to be transported, as yf this our Graunte had not been made nor graunted. AND, Wee doe further will, and by theis Presents, for Vs. our Heires and Successors, firmlie enioine and comaunde, as well the Treasorer, Chauncellor and Barons of the Exchequer, of Vs. our Heires and Successors, as also all and singuler the Customers, Farmors, and Collectors of the Customes, Subsidies, and Imposts and other the Officers and Ministers of Vs our Heires and Successors whatsoever, for the Tyme Being, That they and every of them, vpon the strewing forth vnto them of theis

THE CHARTER OF MASSACHUSETTS BAY: 1629

Letters patents, or the Duplicate or exemplificacon of the same, without any other Writt or Warrant whatsoever from Vs. our Heires or Successors, to be obteyned or sued forth, doe and shall make full, whole, entire, and due Allowance, and cleare Discharge vnto the saide Governor and Company, and their Successors, of all Customes, Subsidies, Imposicons, Taxes and Duties whatsoever, that shall or maie be claymed by Vs. our Heires and Successors, of or from the said Governor and Company, and their Successors, for or by Reason of the said Goodes, Chattels, Wares, Merchandizes, and Premises to be exported out of our saide Domynions, or any of them, into any Parte of the saide Landes or Premises hereby mencoed, to be given, graunted, and confirmed, or for, or by Reason of any of the saide Goodes, Chattells, Wares, or Merchandizes to be imported from the said Landes and Premises hereby mencoed, to be given, graunted, and confirmed into any of our saide Dominions, or any Parte thereof as aforesaide, excepting onlie the saide five Poundes per Centum hereby reserved and payeable after the Expiracon of the saide Terme of seaven Yeares as aforesaid, and not before: And theis our Letters-patents, or the Inrollment, Duplicate, or Exemplificacon of the same shalbe for ever hereafter, from time to tyme, as well to the Treasorer, Chauncellor and Barons of the Exchequer of Vs. our Heires and Successors, as to all and singuler the Customers, Farmors, and Collectors of the Customes, Subsidies, and Imposts of Vs. our Heires and Successors, and all Searchers, and other the Officers and Ministers whatsoever of Vs. our Heires and Successors, for the Time being, a sufficient Warrant and Discharge in this Behalf.

AND, further our Will and Pleasure is, and Wee doe hereby for Vs. our Heires and Successors, ordeyne and declare, and graunte to the saide Governor and Company, and their Successors, That all and every the Subiects of Vs. our Heires or Successors, which shall goe to and inhabite within the saide Landes and Premisses hereby mencoed to be graunted, and every of their Children which shall happen to be borne there, or on the Seas in goeing thither, or returning from thence, shall have and enjoy all liberties and Immunities of free and naturall Subiects within any of the Domynions of Vs. our Heires or Successors, to all Intents, Construccons, and Purposes whatsoever, as yf they and everie of them were borne within the Realme of England. And that the Governor and Deputie Governor of the said Company for the Tyme being, or either of them, and any two or more of such of the saide Assistants as shalbe therevnto appointed by the saide Governor and Companv at any of their Courts or Assemblies to be held as aforesaide, shall and maie at all Tymes, and from tyme to tyme hereafter, have full Power and Authoritie to minister and give the Oathe and Oathes of Supremacie and Allegiance, or either of them, to all and everie Person and Persons, which shall at any Tyme or Tymes hereafter goe or passe to the Landes and Premisses hereby mencoed to be graunted to inhabite in the same. AND, Wee doe of our further Grace, certen Knowledg and meere Mocon, give and graunte to the saide Governor and Companv, and their Successors, That it shall and male be lawfull, to and for the Governor or Deputie Governor, and such of the Assistants and Freemen of the said Company for the Tyme being as shalbe assembled in any of their generall Courts aforesaide, or in any other Courtes to be specially sumoned and assembled for that Purpose, or the greater Parte of them (whereof the Governor or Deputie Governor, and six of the Assistants to be alwaies seaven) from tyme to tyme, to make, ordeine, and establishe all Manner of wholesome and reasonable Orders, Lawes, Statutes, and Ordilmces, Direccons, and Instruccons, not contrairie to the Lawes of this our Realme of England, aswell for selling of the Formes and Ceremonies of Governmt and Magistracy fitt and necessary for the said Plantacon, and the Inhabitants there, and for nameing and setting of all sorts of Officers, both superior and inferior, which they shall finde needefull for that Governement and Plantacon, and the distinguishing and setting forth of the severall duties, Powers, and Lymytts of every such Office and Place, and the Formes of such Oathes warrantable by the Lawes and Statutes of this our Realme of England, as shalbe respectivelie ministred vnto them for the Execucon of the said severall Offices and Places; as also, for the disposing and ordering of the Eleccons of such of the said Officers as shalbe annuall, and of such others as shalbe to succeede in Case of Death or Remove all and ministering the said Oathes to the newe elected Officers, and for Imposicons of lawfull Fynes, Mulcts, Imprisonment, or other lawfull Correccon, according to the Course of other Corporacons in this our Realme of England, and for the directing, ruling, and disposeing of all other Matters and Thinges, whereby our said People, Inhabitants there, may be soe religiously, peaceablie, and civilly governed, as their good Life and orderlie Conversacon, maie wynn and incite the Natives of Country, to the Knowledg and Obedience of the onlie true God and Saulor of Mankinde, and the Christian Fayth, which in our Royall Intencon, and the Adventurers free Profession, is the principall Ende of this Plantacion. WILLING, comaunding, and requiring, and by theis Presents for Vs. our Heiress Successors, ordoyning and appointing, that all such Orders, Lawes, Statuts and Ordinnces, Instruccons and Direccons, as shalbe soe made by the Governor, or Deputie Governor of the said Company, and such of the Assistants and Freemen as aforesaide, and published in Writing, under their comon Seale, shalbe carefullie and duly observed, kept, performed, and putt in Execucon, according to the true Intent and Meaning of the same; and theis our Letters-patents, or the Duplicate or exemplificacon thereof, shalbe to all and everie such Officers,-superior and inferior, from Tyme to Tyme, for the putting of the same Orders, Lawes, Statutes, and Ordinuces, Instruccons, and Direccons, in due Execucon against Vs. our Heires and Successors, a sufficient Warrant and Discharge.

AND WEE DOE further, for Vs. our Heires and Successors, give and graunt to the said Governor and Company, and their Successors bv theis Presents, that all and everie such Chiefe Comaunders, Captaines, Governors, and other Officers and Ministers, as by the said Orders, Lawes, Statuts, Ordinnces, Instruccons, or Direccons of the said Governor and Company for the Tyme being, shalbe from Tyme to Tyme hereafter vmploied either in the Government of the saide Inhabitants and Plantacon, or in the Waye by Sea thither, or from thence, according to the Natures and Lymitts of their Offices and Places respectively, shall from Tyme to Tyme hereafter for ever, within the Precincts and Partes of Newe

England hereby mencoed to be graunted and confirmed, or in the Waye by Sea thither, or from thence, have full and Absolute Power and Authoritie to correct, punishe, pardon, governe, and rule all such the Subiects of Vs. our Heires and Successors, as shall from Tyme to Tyme adventure themselves in any Voyadge thither or from thence, or that shall at any Tyme hereafter, inhabite within the Precincts and Partes of Newe England aforesaid, according to the Orders, Lawes, Ordinnces, Instruccons, and Direccons aforesaid, not being repugnant to the Lawes and Statutes of our Realme of England as aforesaid. AND WEE DOE further, for Vs. our Heires and Successors, give and graunte to the said Governor and Company, and their Successors, by theis Presents, that it shall and maie be lawfull, to and for the Chiefe Comaunders, Governors, and officers of the said Company for the Time being, who shalbe resident in the said Parte of Newe England in America, by theis presents graunted, and others there inhabiting by their Appointment and Direccon, from Tyme to Tyme, and at all Tymes hereafter for their speciall Defence and Safety, to incounter, expulse, repell, and resist by Force of Armes, aswell by Sea as by Lande, and by all fitting Waies and Meanes whatsoever, all such Person and Persons, as shall at any Tyme hereafter, attempt or enterprise the Destruccon, Invasion, Detriment, or Annoyaunce to the said Plantation or Inhabitants, and to take and surprise by all Waies and Meanes whatsoever, all and every such Person and Persons, with their Shippes, Armour, Municons and other Goodes, as shall in hostile manner invade or attempt the defeating of the said Plantacon, or the Hurt of the said Company and Inhabitants: NEVERTHELESS, our Will and Pleasure is, and Wee doe hereby declare to all Christian Kinges, Princes and States, that yf any Person or Persons which shall hereafter be of the said Company or Plantacon or any other by Lycense or Appointment of the said Governor and Company for the Tyme being, shall at any Tyme or Tymes hereafter, robb or spoyle, by Sea or by Land, or doe any Hurt, Violence, or vnlawful Hostilitie to any of the Subjects of Vs. our Heires or Successors, or any of the Subjects of any Prince or State, being then in League and Amytie with Vs. our Heires and Successors, and that upon such injury don and vpon iust Complaint of such Prince or State or their Subjects, WEE, our Heires and Successors shall make open Proclamacon within any of the Partes within our Realme of England, comodious for that purpose, that the Person or Persons haveing comitted any such Roberie or Spoyle, shall within the Terme lymytted by such a Proclamacon, make full Restitucon or Satisfaccon of all such Iniureis don, soe as the said Princes or others so complayning, maie hould themselves fullie satisfied and contented; and that yf the said Person or Persons, haveing comitted such Robbery or Spoile, shall not make, or cause to be made Satisfaccon accordinglie, within such Tyme soe to be lymytted, that then it shalbe lawfull for Vs. our Heires and Successors, to putt the said Person or Persons out of our Allegiance and Proteccon, and that it shalbe lawfull and free for all Princes to prosecute with Hostilitie, the said Offendors, and every of them, their and every of their Procurers, Ayders, Abettors, and Comforters in that Behalf: PROVIDED also, and our expresse Will and Pleasure is, And Wee doe by theis Presents for Vs. our Heires and Successors ordeyne and appoint That theis Presents shall not in any manner envre, or be taken to abridge, barr, or hinder any of our loving subjects whatsoever, to vse and exercise the Trade of Fishing vpon that Coast of New England in America, by theis Presents mencoed to be graunted. But that they, and every, or any of them shall have full and free Power and Liberty to continue and vse their said Trade of Fishing vpon the said Coast, in any the Seas therevnto adioyning, or any Armes of the Seas or Saltwater Rivers where they have byn wont to fishe, and to build and sett vp vpon the Landes by theis Presents graunted, such Wharfes, Stages, and Workehouses as shalbe necessarie for the salting, drying, keeping, and packing vp of their Fish, to be taken or gotten vpon that Coast; and to cutt down, and take such Trees and other Materialls there groweing, or being, or shalbe needefull for that Purpose, and for all other necessarie Easements, Helpes, and Advantage concerning their said Trade of Fishing there, in such Manner and Forme as they have byn heretofore at any tyme accustomed to doe, without making any wilfull Waste or Spoyle, any Thing in theis Presents conteyned to the contrarie notwithstanding. AND WEE DOE further, for Vs. our Heires and Successors, ordeyne and graunte to the said Governor and Company, and their Successors by theis Presents that theis our Letters-patents shalbe firme, good, effectuall, and availeable in all Thinges, and to all Intents and Construccons of Lawe, according to our true Meaning herein before declared, and shalbe construed, reputed, and adjudged in all Cases most favourablie on the Behalf, and for the Benefist and Behoofe of the saide Governor and Company and their Successors: ALTHOUGH expresse mencon of the true yearely Value or certenty of the Premisses or any of them; or of any other Guiftes or Grauntes, by Vs. or any of our Progenitors or Predecessors to the foresaid Governor or Company before this tyme made, in theis-Presents is not made; or any Statute, Acte, Ordinnce, Provision, Proclamacon, or Restrainte to the contrarie thereof, heretofore had, made, published, ordeyned, or provided, or any other Matter, Cause, or Thinge whatsoever to the contrarie thereof in any wise notwithstanding.

IN WITNES whereof, Wee have caused theis our Letters to be made Patents.

WITNES ourself, at Westminster, the fourth day of March, in the fourth Yeare of our Raigne.

Per Breve de Privato Sigillo,

Wolseley.

Praedictus Matthaeus Cradocke Juratus est de Fide et Obedientia Regi et Successoribus suis, et de Debita Executione Officii Guberatoris Juxta Tenorem Praesentium, 18° Martii, 1628. Coram me Carolo Casare Milite in Cancellaria Mro.

CHAR.CAESAR.

The Great Seal of England appendant by a parti-coloured silk string.

Source: Yale Law School The Avalon Project

https://avalon.law.yale.edu/17th_century/mass03.asp

Appendix C
INSCRIPTION FROM 1642 LETTER ON THE FOUNDING OF HARVARD

An excerpt from a 1642 letter on the founding of Harvard is engraved on a tablet affixed to Johnson Gate, an entrance to Harvard University.

> After God had carried us safe to New England, and we had built our houses, provided necessaries for our livelihood, reared convenient places for God's worship, and settled the Civil Government: One of the next things we longed for, and looked after was to advance learning, and perpetuate it to posterity, dreading to leave an illiterate ministry to the churches, when our present ministers shall lie in the dust.

The letter, titled "New England's First Fruits in Respect in the Progress of Learning in the College at Cambridge, in Massachusetts Bay," was written in Boston and dated September 26, 1642. It was published in London in 1643, a year after the graduation of Harvard's first class of nine members.

Appendix D

STUDENT RULES FROM 1642 LETTER ON THE FOUNDING OF HARVARD

1. When any scholar is able to understand Tully, or such like classical Latin author extempore, and make and speak true Latin in verse and prose, And decline perfectly the paradigms of nouns and verbs in the Greek tongue: Let him then and not before be capable of admission into the college.

    2. **Let every student be plainly instructed, and earnestly pressed to consider well, the main end of his life and studies is, to know God and Jesus Christ which is eternal life, John 17.3. and therefore to lay Christ in the bottom, as the only foundation of all sound knowledge and learning.** [emphasis added]

    And seeing the Lord only giveth wisdom, let every one seriously set himself by prayer in secret to seek it of him Prov. 2, 3.

    3. Every one shall so exercise himself in reading the Scriptures twice a day, that he shall be ready to give such an account of his proficiency therein, both in theoretical observations of the language, and logic, and in practical and spiritual truths, as his tutor shall require, according to his ability; seeing the entrance of the word giveth light, it giveth understanding to the simple, Psalm. 119. 130.

    4. That they eschewing all profanation of God's name, attributes, word, ordinance, and times of worship, do study with good conscience, carefully to retain God, and the love of his truth in

their minds else let them know, that (notwithstanding their learning) God may give them up to strong delusions, and in the end to a reprobate mind, 2 Thes. 2. 11, 12. Rom. 1. 28.

5. That they studiously redeem the time; observe the general hours appointed for all the students, and the special hours for their own classes: and then diligently attend the lectures without any disturbance by word or gesture. And if in any thing they doubt, they shall inquire as of their fellows, so, (in case of non satisfaction) modestly of their tutors.

6. None shall under any pretense whatsoever, frequent the company and society of such men as lead an unfit, and desolate life. Nor shall any without his tutor's leave, or (in his absence) the call of parents or guardians, go abroad to other towns.

7. Every scholar shall be present in his tutor's chamber at the seventh hour in the morning, immediately after the sound of the bell, at his opening the Scripture and prayer, so also at the fifth hour at night, and then give account of his own private reading, as aforesaid in particular the third, and constantly attend lectures in the hall at the hours appointed. But if any (without necessary impediment) shall absent himself from prayer or lectures, he shall be liable to admonition, if he offend above once a week.

8. If any scholar shall be found to transgress any of the laws of God, or the school, after twice admonition, he shall be liable, if not adultus, to correction, if adultus, his name shall be given up to the overseers of the college, that he may be admonished at the public monthly act. . .

Source: The letter, titled "New England's First Fruits in Respect in the Progress of Learning in the College at Cambridge, in Massachusetts Bay," was written in Boston and dated September 26, 1642. It was published in London in 1643, a year after the graduation of Harvard's first class of nine members. The letter was reprinted in *America: Great Crises in Our History Told by Its Makers: A Library of Original Sources, Vol II, Colonization, 1562-1753,* Chicago: Veterans of Foreign Wars of the United States, 1925. A PDF copy of the book is on Robert J. Allen's website at https://www.robertjallen.org/2010/03/12/founding-of-harvard-college-documents/

Appendix E
LAWS OF THE MASSACHUSETTS BAY COLONY 1648

(From *The Book of the General Lawes and Libertyes Concerning the Inhabitants of the Massachusets* [1648; facsimile edition, Cambridge: Harvard University Press, 1929]).

[*iii] TO OUR BELOVED BRETHREN AND NEIGHBOURS the Inhabitants of the Massachusets, the Governour, Assistants and Deputies assembled in the Generall Court of that Jurisdiction with grace and peace in our Lord Jesus Christ.

So soon as God had set up Politicall Government among his people Israel he gave them a body of lawes for judgement both in civil and criminal causes. These mere breif and fundamental principles, yet withall so full and comprehensive as out of them clear deductions were to be drawne to all particular cases in future times.

For a Common-wealth without lawes is like a Ship without rigging and steeradge. Nor is it sufficient to have principles or fundamentalls, but these are to be drawn out into so many of their deductions as the time and condition of that people may have use of. And it is very unsafe & injurious to the body of the people to put them to learn their duty and libertie from generall rules, nor is it enough to have lawes except they be also just. Therefore among other priviledges which the Lord bestowed upon his peculiar people, these he calls them specially to consider of, that God was neerer to them and their lawes were more righteous then other nations. God was sayd to be amongst them or neer to them because of his Ordnances established by himselfe, and their lawes righteous because himselfe was their Law-giver: yet in the comparison are implyed two things, first that other nations had somthing of God's presence amongst them. Secondly that there was also some what of equitie in their lawes, for it pleased the Father (upon the Covenant of Redemption with his Son) to restore so much of his Image to lost man as whereby all nations are disposed to worship God, and to advance righteousnes: which appears in that of the Apostle Rom. I. 21. They knew God &c: and in the 2. 14. They did by nature the things conteined in the law of God. But the nations corrupting his Ordinances (both of Religion, and Justice) God withdrew his presence from them proportionably whereby they were given up to abominable lusts Rom. 2. 21. Whereas if they had walked according to the light & law of nature they might have been preserved from such moral evils and might have injoyed a common blessing in all their natural and civil Ordinances: now, if it might have been so with the nations who were so much strangers to the Covenant of Grace, what advantage have they who have interest in this Covenant, and may injoye the special presence of God in the puritie and native simplicitie of all his Ordinances by which he is so neer to his owne people. This hath been no small priviledge, and advantage to us in New England that our Churches, and civil State have been planted, and growne up (like two twinnes) together like that of Israel in the wildernes by which wee were put in minde (and had opportunitie put into our hands) not only to gather our Churches, and set up the Ordinaces of Christ Jesus in them according to the Apostolick patterne by such light as the Lord graciously afforded us: but also withall to frame our civil Politie, and lawes according to the rules of his most holy word whereby each do help and strengthen other (the Churches the civil Authoritie, and the civil Authoritie the Churches) and so both prosper the better without such amulation, and contention for priviledges or priority as have proved the misery (if not ruine) of both in some other places.

APPENDIX E

For this end about nine years since wee used the help of some of the Elders of our Churches to compose a modell of the Judiciall lawes of Moses with such other cases as might be referred to them, with intent to make use of them in composing our lawes, but not to have them published as the lawes of this Jurisdiction: nor were they voted in Court. For that book intitled The Liberties &c: published about seven years since (which conteines also many lawes and orders both for civil & criminal causes, and is commonly (though without ground) reported to be our Fundamentalls that wee owne as established by Authoritie of this Court, and that after three year experience & generall approbation: and accordingly we have inserted them into this volume under the severall heads to which they belong yet not as fundamentalls, for diversof them have since been repealed, or altered, and more may justly be (at least) amended heerafter as further experience shall discover defects or inconveniences for Nihil fimul natum et perfectum. [*iv]

The same must we say of this present Volume, we have not published it as a perfect body of laws sufficient to carry on the Government established for future times, nor could it be expected that we should promise such a thing. For if it be no disparagement to the wisedome of that High Court of Parliament in England that in four hundred years they could not so compile their lawes, and regulate proceedings in Courts of justice &c: but that they had still new work to do of the same kinde almost every Parliament: there can be no just cause to blame a poor Colonie (being unfurnished of Lawyers and Statesmen) that in eighteen years hath produced no more, nor better rules for a good, and setled Government then this Book holds forth: nor have you (our Bretheren and Neighbours) any cause, whether you look back upon our Native Country, or take your observation by other States, & Common wealths in Europe) to complaine of such as you have imployed in this service; for the time which hath been spent in making lawes, and repealing and altering them so often, nor of the charge whicht he Country hath been put to for those occasions, the Civilian gives you a satisfactorie reason of such continuall alterations additions &c: Crefcit in Orbe dolus.

These Lawes which were made successively in divers former years, we have reduced under severall heads in an alphabeticall method, that so they might the more readilye be found, & that the divers lawes concerning one matter being placed together the scope and intent of the whole and of every of them might the more easily be apprehended: we must confesse we have not been so exact in placing every law under its most proper title as we might, and would have been: the reason was our hasty indeavour to satisfie your longing expectation, and frequent ecomplaints for want of such a volume to be published in print: wherin (upon every occasion) you might readily see the rule which you ought to walke by. And in this (we hope) you will finde satisfaction, by the help of the references under the severall heads, and the Table which we have added in the end. For such lawes and orders as are not of generall concernment we have not put them into this booke, but they remain still in force, and are to be seen in the booke of the Records of the Court, but all generall laws not heer inserted nor mentioned to be still of force are to be accounted repealed.

You have called us from amongst the rest of our Bretheren and given us power to make these laws: we must now call upon you to see them executed: remembring that old & true proverb, The execution of the law is the life of the law. If one sort of you viz: non-Freemen should object that you had no hand in calling us to this worke, and therfore think yourselvs not bound to obedience &c. Wee answer that a subsequent, or implicit consent is of like force in this case, as an expresse precedent power: for in putting your persons and estates into the protection and way of subsistance held forth and exercised within this Jurisdiction, you doe tacitly submit to this Government and to all the wholesome lawes therof, and so is the common repute in all nations and that upon this Maxim. Qui sentit commodum sentire debet et onus.

If any of you meet with some law that seemes not to tend to your particular benefit, you must consider that lawes are made with respect to the whole people, and not to each particular person: and obedience to them must be yeilded with respect to the common welfare, not to thy private advantage, and as thou yeildest obedience to the law for common good, but to thy dis-advantage: so another must observe some other law for thy good, though to his own damage; thus must we be content to bear õanothers burden and so fullfill the Law of Christ.

That distinction which is put between the Lawes of God and the lawes of men, becomes a snare to many as it is mis-applyed in the ordering of their obedience to civil Authoritie; for when the Authoritie is of God and that in way of an Ordinance Rom. 13. I. and when the administration of it is according to deductions, and rules gathered from the word of God, and the clear light of nature in civil nations, surely there is no humane law that tendeth to commõn good (according to those principles) but the same is mediately a law of God, and that in way of an Ordinance which all are to submit unto and that for conscience sake. Rom. 13. 5.

By order of the Generall Court.

INCREASE NOWEL

SECR.

*[1] THE BOOK OF THE GENERAL LAUUES AND LIBERTYES CONCERNING & c.

FORASMUCH as the free fruition of such Liberties, Immunities, priviledges as humanitie, civilitie & christianity call for as due to everie man in his place, & proportion, without impeachment & infringement hath ever been, & ever will be the tranquility & stability of Churches & Comon-wealths; & the deniall or deprivall therof the disturbance, if not ruine of both:

It is therefore ordered by this Court, & Authority therof, That no mans life shall be taken away; no mans honour or good name shall be stayned; no mans person shal be arrested, restrained, bannished, dismembred nor any wayes punished; no man shall be deprived of his wife or children; no mans goods or estate shal be taken away from him; nor any wayes indamaged under colour of Law or countenance of Authoritie unles it be by the vertue or equity of some espresse law of the Country warranting the same established by a General Court & sufficiently published; or in case of the defect of a law in any particular case by the word of God. And in capital cases, or in cases excōmunicate, condemned or other, shall have full power and libertie to make their Wills & Testaments & other lawfull Alienations of their lands and estates.[1641] see children.

Actions.

All Actions of debt, accounts, slaunder, and Actions of the case concerning debts and accounts shall henceforth be tryed where the Plaintiffe pleaseth; so it be in the jurisdiction of that Court where the Plantiffe, or Defendant dwelleth: unles by consent under both their hands it appeare they would have the case tryed in any other Court. All other Actions shal be tryed within that jurisdiction where the cause of the Action doth arise. [1642]

2 It is ordered by this Court & Authoritie therof, That every person impleading another in any court of Assistants, or County court shal pay the sum of ten shillings before his case be entred, vnles the court see cause to admit any to sue in forma pauperis. [1642]

3 It is ordered by the Authority aforesayd, That where the debt or damage recovered shall amount to ten pounds in every such case to pay five shillings more, and where it shall amount to twenty pounds or upward there to pay ten shillings more then the first ten shillings, which sayd additions shall be put to the Judgement and Execution to be levied by the Marshall and accounted for to the Treasurer. [1647]

4 In all actions brought to any court the Plantiffe shall have liberty to withdraw his action or to be non-suted before the Jurie have given in their verdict; in which case he shall alwayes pay full cost and charges to the Defendant, and may afterward renew his sute at another Court. [1641] see Causes. see Records.

Age.

It is ordered by this Court & the Authoritie therof, that the age for passing away of lands, or such kinde of hereditaments, or for giving of votes, verdicts or sentences in any civil courts or causes, shall be twenty and one years: but in case of chusing of Guardions, fourteen years. [1641 1647]

Ana-Baptists.

Forasmuch as experience hath plentifully & often proved that since the first arising of the Ana-baptists about a hundred years past they have been the Incendiaries of Common-wealths & the Infectors of persons in main matters of Religiõ, & the Troublers of Churches in most places where they have been, & that they who have held the baptizing of Infants unlawful, have usually held other errors or heresies together therwith (though as hereticks use to doe they have concealed the same untill they espied a fit advantage and opportunity to vent them by way of question or scruple) and wheras divers [*2] of this kinde have since our cõming into New-England appeared amongst ourselvs, some wherof as others before them have denied the Ordinance of Magistracy, and the law fulnes of making warre, others the lawfulness of Magistrates, and their Inspection into any breach of the first Table: which opinions if coñived at by us are like to be increased among us & so necessarily bring guilt upõ us, infection, & trouble to the Churches & hazzard to the whole Common-wealth:

It is therfore orderd by this Court & Authoritie therof, that if any person or persons within this Jurisdiction shall either openly condemn or oppose the baptizing of Infants, or goe about secretely to seduce others from the approbation or use therof, or shal purposely depart the Congregation at the administration of that Ordinance; or shal deny the Ordinance of Magistry, or their lawfull right or authoritie to make war, or to punish the outward breaches of the first Table, and shall appear to the Court wilfully and obstinately to continue therin, after due meanes of conviction, everie such person or persons shall be sentenced to Banishment. [1644] * * *

Arrests.

It is ordered and decreed by this Court & Authoritie therof, That no mans person shall be arrested or imprisoned for any debt or fine if the law can finde any competent meanes of satisfaction otherwise from his estate. And if not his person may be arrested and imprisoned, where he shall be kept at his own charge, not the Plaintiffs, till satisfaction be made; unles the Court that had cognisance of the cause or some superiour Court shall otherwise determine: provided neverthelesse that no mans person shall be kept in prison for debt but when there appears some estate which he will not [*3] produce, to which end any Court or Commissioners authorized by the General Court may administer an oath to the partie or any others suspected to be privie in concealing his estate, but shall satisfie by service if the Creditor require it but shall not be solde to any but of the English nation. [1641: 1647] see sect 1. page 1. * * *

Bakers.

It is ordered by this Court and Authoritie therof, that henceforth every Baker shall have a distinct mark for his bread, & keep the true assizes as heerafter is expressed viz. When wheat is ordinarily sold and these severall rates heerafter mentioned the peñi white loaf by averdupois weight shall weigh when wheat is by the bushell at 3 ss. od. The white 11 ouces 1 gr wheaten 17 ouc. 1 gr. Houshould 23 ouc. o.

at 3	6	10	1	15	1	20	2.
at 4	0	09	1	14	0	18	2.
at 4	6	08	1	11	3	16	2.
at 5	0	07	3	11	2	15	2.
at 5	6	07	0	10	2	14	0.
at 6	0	06	2	10	0	13	0.
at 6	6	06	0	09	2	12	2.

and so proportionably: under the penaltie of forfeiting all such bread as shall not be of the severall assizes as is aforementioned to the use of the poor of the towne where the offence is committed, and otherwise as is heerafter expressed: and for the better execution of this present Order; there shall be in everie market towne, and all other townes needfull, one or two able persons annually chosen by each towne, who shall be sworn at the next county Court. or by the next Magistrate, unto the faithfull discharge of his or their office;

who are heerby authorized to enter into all houses, either with a Constable or without where they shall suspect or be informed of any bread baked for sale: & also to weigh the said bread as oft as they see cause: and to seize all such as they finde defective. As also to weigh all butter made up for sale; and bringing unto, or being in the towne or market to be solde by weight: which if found light after notice once given shall be forfeited in like manner. The like penaltie shall be for not marking all bread made for sale. and the sayd officer shall have one third part of all forfeitures for his paines; the rest to the poor as aforesayd. [1646]

[*4] Bills.

It is ordered by the Authority of this Court that any debt, or debts due upon bill, or other specialtie assigned to another; shall be as good a debt & estate to the Assignee as it was to the Assigner at the time of it's assignation. And that it shall be lawfull for the sayd Assignee to sue for and recover the said debt, due upon bill, and so assigned, as fully as the originall creditor might have done, provided the said assignement be made upon the backside of the bill or specialtie. [1647] see usurie. Bond-slavery.

It is ordered by this Court and authoritie therof, that there shall never be any bond-slavery, villenage or captivitie amongst us; unlesse it be lawfull captives, taken in just warrs, and such strangers as willingly sell themselves, or are solde to us: and such shall have the libertyes and christian usages which the law of God established in Israell concerning such persons doth morally require, provided, this exempts none from servitude who shall be judged thereto by Authoritie. [1641] * * *

Burglarie and Theft.

Forasmuch as many persons of late years have been, and are apt to be injurious to the goods and lives of others, notwithstanding all care and meanes to prevent and punish the same; - - -

It is therefore ordered by this Court and Authoritie therof that if any person shall commit Burglarie by breaking up any dwelling house, or shall rob any person in the field, or high wayes; such a person so offending shall for the first offence be branded on the forehead with the letter (B) If he shall offend in the same kinde the second time, he shall be branded as before and also be severally whipped: and if he shall fall into the like offence the third time he shall be put to death, as being incorrigible. And if any person shal commit such Burglarie, or rob in the fields or house on the Lords day [*5] besides the former punishments, he shal for the first offence have one of his ears cut off. And for the second offence in the same kinde he shal loose his other ear in the same maner. And if he fall into the same offence a third time he shal be put to death if it appear to the Court he did it presumptously. [1642 1647]

2 For the prevention of Pilfring and Theft, it is ordered by this Court and Authoritie therof; that if any person shal be taken or known to rob any orchard or garden, that shall hurt, or steal away any grafts or fruit trees, fruits, linnen, woollen, or any other goods left out in orchards, gardens, backsides, or any other place in house or fields: or shall steal any wood or other goods from the waterside, from mens doors, or yards; he shall forfeit treble damage to the owners therof. And if they be children, or servants that shall trespasse heerin, if their parents or masters will not pay the penaltie before expressed, they shal be openly whipped. And forasmuch as many times it so falls out that small thefts and other offences of a criminall nature, are committed both by English & Indian, in townes remote from any prison, or other fit place to which such malefactors may be committed till the next Court, it is therfore heerby ordered; that any Magistrate upon complaint made to him may hear, and upon due proof determin any small offences of the aforesayed nature, according to the laws heer established, and give warrant to the Constable of that town where the offender lives to levie the same: provided the damage or fine exceed not fourty shillings: provided also it shall be lawfull for either partie to appeal to the next Court to be holden in that Jurisdiction, giving sufficient caution to prosecute the same to effect at the said Court. And everie Magistrate shall make return yearly to the Court of Jurisdiction, wherin he liveth of what cases he hath so ended. And also the Constables of all such fines as they have received. And

APPENDIX E

where the offender hath nothing to satisfie such Magistrate may punish by stocks, or whipping as the cause shall deserve, not exceeding ten stripes. It is also ordered that all servants & workmen imbeazling the goods of their masters, or such as set them on work that make restitution and be lyable to all lawes & penalties as other men. [1646]

CAPITAL LAWES.

IF any man after legal conviction shall HAVE OR WORSHIP any other God, but the LORD GOD: he shall be put to death. Exod. 22. 20. Deut. 13. 6. & 10. Deut. 17. 2. 6.

2. If any man or woman be a WITCH, that is, hath or consulteth with a familiar spirit, they shall be put to death. Exod. 22. 18. Levit. 20. 27. Deut. 18. 10. 11.

3. If any person within this Jurisdiction whether Christian or Pagan shall wittingly and willingly presume to BLASPHEME the holy Name of God, Father, Son or Holy-Ghost, with direct, expresse, presumptuous, or high-handed blasphemy, either by wilfull or obstinate denying the true God, or his Creation, or Government of the world: or shall curse God in like manner, or reproach the holy Religion of God as if it were but a politick device to keep ignorant men in awe; or shal utter any other kinde of Blasphemy of the like nature & degree they shall be put to death. Levit. 24, 15. 16.

4. If any person shall commit any wilfull MURTHER, which is Man slaughter, committed upon premeditate malice, hatred, or crueltie not in a mans necessary and just defence, nor by meer casualty against his will, he shall be put to death. Exod. 21. 12. 13. Numb. 35. 31.

5. If any person slayeth another suddenly in his ANGER, or CRUELTY of passion, he shall be put to death. Levit. 24. 17. Numb. 35. 20. 21.

6. If any person shall slay another through guile, either by POYSONING, or other such develish practice, he shall be put to death. Exod. 21. 14.

7. If any man or woman shall LYE WITH ANY BEAST, or bruit creature, by carnall copulation; they shall surely be put to death: and the beast shall be slain, & buried, and not eaten. Lev. 20, 15. 16.

8. If any man LYETH WITH MAN-KINDE as he lieth with a woman, both of them have committed abomination, they both shal surely be put to death: unles the one partie were forced (or be under fourteen years of age in which case he shall be seveerly [*6] punished) Levit. 20. 13.

9. If any person commit ADULTERIE with a married, or espoused wife; the Adulterer & Adulteresse shal surely be put to death. Lev. 20. 19. & 18. 20. Deu. 22. 23. 27.

10. If any man STEALETH A MAN, or Man-kinde, he shall surely be put to death. Exodus 21. 16.

11. If any man rise up by FALSE-WITNES wittingly, and of purpose to take away any mans life: he shal be put to death. Deut. 19. 16. 18. 16.

12. If any man shall CONSPIRE, and attempt any Invasion, Insurrection, or publick Rebellion against our Common-Wealth: or shall indeavour to surprize any Town, or Townes, Fort, or Forts therin; or shall treacherously, & persidiously attempt the Alteration and Subversion of our frame of Politie, or Government fundamentally he shall be put to death. Numb. 16. 2 Sam. 3. 2 Sam. 18. 2 Sam. 20.

13. If any child, or children, above sixteen years old, and of sufficient understanding, shall CURSE, or SMITE their natural FATHER, or MOTHER; he or they shall be put to death: unles it can be sufficiently testified that the Parents have been very unchristianly negligent in the eduction of such children; or so provoked them by extream, and cruel correction; that they have been forced therunto to preserve themselves from death or maiming. Exod. 21. 17. Lev. 20. 9. Exod. 21. 15.

14. If a man have a stubborn or REBELLIOUS SON, of sufficient years & uderstanding (viz) sixteen years of age, which will not obey the voice of his Father, or the voice of his Mother, and that

APPENDIX E

when they have chastened him will not harken unto them: then shal his Father & Mother being his natural parets, lay hold on him, & bring him to the Magistrates assembled in Court & testifie unto them that their Son is stubborn & rebellious & will not obey their voice and chastisement, but lives in sundry notorious crimes, such a son shal be put to death. Deut. 21. 20. 21.

15. If any man shal RAVISH any maid or single womãn, cõmitting carnal copulation with her by force, against her own will; that is above the age of ten years he shal be punished either with death, or with some other greivous punishmet according to circumstances as the Judges, or General court shal determin. [1641]

Cask & Cooper.

It is orderedy by this Court and authoritie therof, that all cask used for any liquor, fish, or other cõmoditie to be put to sale shall be of London assize, and that fit persons shal be appointed from time to time in all places needfull, to gage all such vessels or cask & such as shal be found of due assize shal be marked with the Gagers mark, & no other who shal have for his paines four pence for every tun, & so proportionably. And every County court or any one Magistrate upon notice given them shall appoint such Gagers to view the said cask, & to see that they be right, & of sound & wel seasoned timber, & that everie Cooper have a distinct brand-mark on his own cask, upon payn of forfeiture of twenty shilling in either case, & so proportiõably for lesser vessels. [1642 1647] * * *

[*23] Fornication.

It is ordered by this Court and Authoritie therof, That if any man shall commit Fornication with any single woman, they shall be punished either by enjoyning to Marriage, or Fine, or corporall punishment, or all or any of these as the Judges in the courts of Assistants shall appoint most agreeable to the word of God. And this Order to continue till the Court take further order. [1642] * * *

[*24] Gaming.

UPON complaint of great disorder by the use of the game called Shuffle-board, in houses of common entertainment, wherby much pretious time is spent unfruitfully and much wast of wine and beer occasioned, it is therfore ordered and enacted by the Authoritie of this Court;

That no person shall henceforth use the said game of Shuffle-board in any such house, nor in any other house used as common for such purpose, upon payn for every Keeper of such house to forfeit for every such offence twenty shillings: and for every person playing at the said game in any such house, to forfeit for everie such offence five shillings: Nor shall any person at any time play or game for any monie, or mony-worth upon penalty of forfeiting treble the value therof: one half to the partie informing, the other half to the Treasurie. And any Magistrate may hear and determin any offence against this Law. [1646 1647] * * *

Heresie. ALTHOUGH no humane power be Lord over the Faith & Consciences of men, and therfore may not constrein them to beleive or professe against their Consciences: yet because such as bring in damnable heresies, tending to the subversion of the Christian Faith, and destruction of the soules of men, ought duly to be restreined from such notorious impiety, it is therfore ordered and decreed by this Court;

That if any Christian within this Jurisdiction shall go about to subvert and destroy the christian Faith and Religion, by broaching or mainteining any damnable heresie; as denying the immortalitie of the Soul, or the resurrection of the body, or any sin to be repented of in the Regenerate, or any evil done by the outward man to be accounted sin: or denying that Christ gave himself a Ransom for our sins, or shal affirm that wee are not justified by his Death and Righteousnes, but by the perfection of our own works; or shall deny the moralitie of the fourth commandement, or shall indeavour to seduce others to any the herisies aforementioned, everie such person continuing obstinate therin after due means of conviction shal be sentenced to Bañishment. [1646] * * *

[*25] Idlenes.

APPENDIX E

It is ordered by this Court and Authoritie therof, that no person, Housholder or other shall spend his time idlely or unproffitably under pain of such punishment as the Court of Assistants or County Court shall think meet to inflict. And for [*26]this end it is ordered that the Constable of everie place shall use speciall care and diligence to take knowledge of offenders in this kinde, especially of common coasters, unproffitable fowlers and tobacco takers, and present the same unto the two next Assistants, who shall have power to hear and determin the cause, or transfer it to the next Court. [1633]

Jesuits.

THIS Court taking into consideration the great wars, combustions and divisions which are this day in Europe: and that the same are observed to be raysed and fomented chiefly by the secret underminings, and solicitations of those of the Jesuiticall Order, men brought up and devoted to the religion and court of Rome; which hath occasioned divers States to expell them their territories; for prevention wherof among our selves, It is ordered and enacted by Authoritie of this Court,

That no Jesuit, or spiritual or ecclesiastical person [as they are termed] ordained by the authoritie of the Pope, or Sea of Rome shall henceforth at any time repair to, or come within this Jurisdiction: And if any person shal give just cause of suspicion that he is one of such Societie or Order he shall be brought before some of the Magistrates, and if he cannot free himselfe of such suspicion he shall be committed to prison, or bound over to the next Court of Assistants, to be tryed and proceeded with by Bañishment or otherwise as the Court shall see cause: and if any person so banished shall be taken the second time within this Jurisdiction upon lawfull tryall and conviction he shall be put to death. Provided this Law shall not extend to any such Jesuit, spiritual or ecclesiasticall person as shall be cast upon our shoars, by ship-wrack or other accident, so as he continue no longer then till he may have opportunitie of passage for his departure; nor to any such as shall come in company with any Messenger hither upõ publick occasions, or any Merchant or Master of any ship, belonging to any place not in emnitie with the State of England, or our selves, so as they depart again with the same Messenger, Master of Merchant, and behave themselves in-offensively during their aboad heer. [1647] * * *

[*29] In-keepers, Tippling, Drunkenes.

Forasmuch as there is a necessary use of houses of common entertainment in every Common-wealth, and of such as retail wine, beer and victuals; yet because there are so many abuses of that lawfull libertie, both by persons entertaining and persons entertained, there is also need of strict Laws and Rules to regulate such an employment: It is therefore ordered by this Court and Authoritie thereof;

[* 30]

That no person or persons shall at any time under any pretence or colour whatsoever undertake to be a common Victuailer, Keeper of a Cooks shop or house for common entertainment, Taverner, or publick seller of wine, ale, beer or strongwater (by re-tale) nor shall any sell wine privately in his house or out of doors by a lesse quantitie or under a quarter cask: without approbation of the selected Townsmen and Licence of the Shire Court where they dwell: upon pain of forfeiture of five pounds for everie such offence, or imprisonment at pleasure of the Court, where satisfaction cannot be had.

And every person so licenced for common entertainment shall have some inoffensive Signe obvious for strangers direction, and such as have no such Signe after three months so licenced from time to time shall lose their licence: and others allowed in their stead. And any licenced person that selleth beer shall not sell any above two-pence the ale-quart: upon penaltie of three shillings four pence for everie such offence. And it is permitted to any that will to sell beer out of doors at a pennie the ale-quart and under.

Neither shall any such licenced person aforesaid suffer any to be drunken, or drink excessively viz: above half a pinte of wine for one person at one time; or to continue tippling above the space of half an hour, or at unreasonable times, or after nine of the clock at night in, or about any of their houses on penaltie of five shillings for everie such offence.

And everie person found drunken viz: so that he be thereby bereaved or disabled in the use of his understanding, appearing in his speech or gesture in any of the said houses or elsewhere shall forfeit ten shillings. And for excessive drinking three shillings four pence. And for continuing above half an hour tippling two shillings six pence. And for tippling at unreasonable times, or after nine a clock at night five shillings: for everie offence in these particulars being lawfully convict thereof. And for want of payment such shall be imprisoned untill they pay: or be set in the Stocks one hour or more [in some open place] as the weather will permit not exceeding three hours at one time.

Provided notwithstanding such licenced persons may entertain sea-faring men, or land travellers in the night-season, when they come first on shore, or from their journy for their necessarie refreshment, or when they prepare for their voyage or journie the next day early; so there be no disorder among them; and also Strangers, Lodgers or other persons in an orderly way may continue in such houses of common entertainment during meal times, or upon lawfull busines what time their occasions shall require.

Nor shall any Merchant, Cooper, Owner or Keeper of wines or other persons that have the government of them suffer any person to drink to excesse, or drunkenes, in any their wine-Cellars, Ships or other vessels or places where wines doe lye; on pain to forfeit for each person so doing ten shillings.

And if any person offend in drunkenes, excessive or long drinking the secŏd time they shall pay double Fines. And if they fall into the same offence the third time they shall pay treble Fines. And if the parties be not able to pay the Fines then he that is found drunk shall be punished by whipping to the number of ten stripes: and he that offends in excessive or long drinking shall be put into the stocks for three hours when the weather may not hazzard his life or lims. And if they offend the fourth time they shall be imprisoned until they put in two sufficient Sureties for their good behaviour.

And it is father ordered that if any person that keepeth or hereafter shall keep a common house of entertainmen, shall be lawfully convicted the third time for any offence against this Law: he shall (for the space of three years next ensuing the said conviction) be disabled to keep any such house of entertainment, or sell wine, beer or the like; unles the Court aforesaid shall see cause to continue them.

It is farther ordered that everie In-keeper, or Victuailer shall provide for the entertainment [* 31] of strangers horses viz: one or more inclosures for Summer and hay and provender for Winters with convenient stable room and attendance under penaltie of two shillings six pence for everie dayes default, and double damage to the partie thereby wronged (except it be by inevitable accident.

And it is farther ordered by the Authoritie aforesaid, that no Taverner or seller of wine by retale, licenced as aforesaid shall take above nine ponds profit by the Butt or Pipe of wine (and proportionably for all other vessels) toward his wast in drawing and otherwise: out of which allowance everie such Taverner or Vintner shall pay fifty shillings by the Butt or Pipe and proportionably for all other vessels to the Countrie. For which he shall account with the Auditor general or his Deputie every six months and discharge the same. All which they may doe by selling six pence a quart in re-tale (which they shall no time exceed) more than it cost by the Butt, beside the benefit of their art and mysterie which they know how to make use of. And everie Taverner or Vintner shall give a true account and notice unto the Auditor or his Deputie of everie vessel of wine he buies from time to time within three daye; upon pain of forfeiting the same or the value thereof.

And all such as retale strong waters shall pay in like manners two pence upon everie quart to the use of the Country, who also shall give notice to the Auditor or his Deputies of everie case and bottle or other quantitie they buy within three dayes upon payn of forfeiture as before.

APPENDIX E

Also it is ordered that in all places where week day Lectures are kept, all Taverners, Victuailers and Tablers that are within a mile of the Meeting-house, shall from time to time clear their houses of all persons able to goe to the Meeting, during the time of the exercise (except upon extraordinary cause, for the necessarie refreshing of strangers unexpectedly repairing to them) upō pain of five shillings for every such offence over and besides the penalties incurred by this Law for any other disorder.

It is also ordered that all offences against this Law may be heard and determined by any one Magistrate, who shall heerby have power by Warrant to fend for parties, and witnesses, and to examin the said witnesses upon oath and the parties without oath, concerning any of these offences: and upon due conviction either by view of the said Magistrate, or affirmation of the Constable, and one sufficient witnes with circumstances concurring, or two witnesses, or confession of the partie to levie the said severall fines, by Warrant to the Constable for that end, who shall be accountable to the Auditor for the same.

And if any person shall voluntarily confesse his offence against this Law in any the particulars thereof, his oath shall be taken in evidence and stand good against any other offending at the same time.

Lastly, it is ordered by the Authoritie aforesaid that all Constables may, and shall from time to time duly make search throughout the limits of their towns upon Lords dayes, and Lecture dayes, in times of Exercise; and also at all other times, so oft as they shall see cause for all offences and offenders against this Law in any of the pariculars thereof. And if upon due information, or complaint of any of their Inhabitants, or other credible persons whether Taverner, Uictuailer, Tabler or other; they shall refuse or neglect to make search as aforesaid, or shall not to their power perform all other things belonging to their place and Office of Constableship: then upon complaint and due proof before any one Magistrate within three months after such refusall or neglect; they shall be fined for everie such offence ten shillings, to be levied by the Marshal as in other cases by Warrant from such Magistrate before whom they are convicted, or Warrant from the treasurer upon notice from such Magistrate. [1645 1646 1647] See Gaming, Licences. ***

[*35] Lying.

Whereas truth in words as well as in actions is required of all men, especially of Chistians who are the professed Servants of the God to Truth; and wheras all lying is contrary to truth, and some sorts of lyes are not only sinfull (as all lyes are) but also pernicious to the Public-weal, and injurious to particular persons; it is therfore ordered by this Court and Authoritie therof,

That everie person of the age of discretion [which is accounted fourteen years] who shall wittingly and willingly make, or publish any Lye which may be pernicious to the publick weal, or tending to the damage or injurie of any particular person, or with intent to

deceive and abuse the people with false news or reports: and the same duly proved in any Court or before any one Magistrate (who hath heerby power graunted to hear, and determin all offences against this Law) such person shall be fined for the first offence ten shillings, or if the partie be unable to pay the same then to be set in the stocks so long as the said Court or Magistrate shall appoint, in some open place, not exceeding two hours. For the second offence in that kinde wherof any shall be legally convicted the sum of twenty shillings, or be whipped upon the naked body not exceeding ten stripes. And for the third offence that way fourty shillings, or if the partie be unable to pay, then to be whipped with more stripes, not exceeding fifteen. And if yet any shall offend in like kinde, and be legally convicted therof, such person, male or female, shall be fined ten shillings a time more then formerly: or if the partie so offending be unable to pay, then to be whipped with five, or six more stripes then formerly not exceeding fourty at any time.

The aforesaid fines shall be levied, or stripes inflicted either by the Marshal of that Jurisdiction, or Constable of the Town where the offence is committed [*36] according as the Court or Magistrate shall direct. And such fines so levied shall be paid to the Treasurie of that Shire where the Cause is tried.

And if any person shall find himselfe greived with the sentence of any such Magistrate out of Court, he may appeal to the next Court of the same Shire, giving sufficient securitie to prosecute his appeal and abide the Order of the Court. And if the said Court shall judge his appeal causlesse, he shall be double fined and pay the charges of the Court during his Action, or corrected by whipping as aforesaid not exceeding fourtie stripes; and pay the costs of Court and partie complaining or informing, and of Wittnesses in the Case.

And for all such as being under age if discretion that shall offend in lying contrary to this Order their Parents or Masters shall give them due correction, and that in the presence of some Officer if any Magistrate shall so appoint. Provided also that no person shall be barred of his just Action of Slaunder, or otherwise by any proceeding upon this Order. [1645] ***

[*38] Masters, Servants, Labourers

1. It is ordered by this Court and the Authoritie therof, that no servant, either man or maid shall either give, sell or truck any commoditie whatsoever without licence from their Masters, during the time of their service under pain of Fine, or corporal punishment at the discretion of the Court as the offence shall deserve.

2. And that all workmen shall work the whole day allowing convenient time for food and rest.

3. It is also ordered that when any servants shall run from their masters, or any other Inhabitants shall privily goe away with suspicion of ill intentions, it shall be lawfull for the next Magistrate, or the Constable and two of the chief Inhabitants where no Magistrate is to presse men and boats or pinnaces at the publick charge to pursue such persons by Sea or Land and ring them back by force of Arms.

4. It is also ordered by the Authoritie aforesaid, that the Free-men of everie town may from time to time as occasion shall require agree amongst themselves about the prizes, and rates of all workmens

labours and servants wages. And everie person inhabiting in any town, whether workman, labourer or servant shall be bound to the same rates which the said Freemen, or the greater part shall binde themselves unto: and whosoever shall exceed those rates so agreed shall be punished by the discretion of the Court of that Shire, according to the qualitie and measure of the offence. And if any town shall have cause of complaint against the Freemen of any other town for allowing greater rates, or wages then themselves, the Quarter Court of that Shire shall from time to time set order therin.

5. And for servants and workmens wages, it is ordered, that they may be paid in corn, to be valued by two indifferent Freemen, chosen the one by the Master, the other by the servant or workman, who also are to have respect to the value of the work or service, and if they cannot agree then a third man shall be chosen by the next Magistrate, or if no Magistrate be in the town then by the next Constable, unles the parties agree the price themselves. Provided if any servant or workman agree for any [*39] particular payment, then to be payd in specie, or consideration for default therin. And for all other payments in corn, if the parties cannot agree they shall choos two indifferent men, and if they cannot agree then a third as before.

6. It is ordered, and by this Court declared, that if any servant shall flee from the tyrannie and crueltie of his, or her Master to the house of any Freeman of the same town, they shall be there protected and susteined till due order be taken for their releif. Provided due notice therof be speedily given to their Master from whom they fled, and to the next Magistrate or Constable where the partie so fled is harboured.

7. Also that no servant shall be put off for above a year to any other, neither in the life time of their Master, nor after their death by their Exectuors or Administrators, unles it be by consent of Authorite assembled in some Court, or two Assistants: otherwise all, and everie such Assignment to be void in Law.

APPENDIX E

8. And that if any man smite out the eye, or tooth of his manservant, or maid-servant; or otherwise maim, or much disfigure them (unles it be by meer casualtie) he shall let them goe free from his service, and shall allow such farther recompence as the Court shall adjudge him.

9. And all servants that have served diligently and faithfully to the benefit of their Masters seven years shall not be sent away emptie: and if any have been unfaithfull, negligent, or unprofitable in their service, notwithstanding the good usage of their Masters, they shall not be dismissed till they have made satisfaction according to the judgement of Authoritie. [1630 1633 1635 1636 1641] see Oppression. ***

[*44] Pipe-staves.

Whereas information hath come to this Court from divers forrein parts of the insufficiencie of our Pipe-staves in regard especially of worm holes, wherby the commoditie is like to be prohibited in those parts, to the great damage of the Countrie; it is therfore ordered and enacted by the Authoritie of this Court,

That the Select-men of Boston and Charlstown, and of all other towns in this Jurisdiction where Pipe-staves use to be shipped; shall forthwith, and so from time to time as need shall require nominate two men of each town, skilfull in that commoditie, and such as can attend that service to be Viewers of Pipe-staves; who so chosen, shall by the Constable be convented before some Magistrate, to be sworn dilligently and faithfully to vie and search all such Pipe-staves as are to be transported to any parts of Spain, Portugal, or within either of their Dominions, or elsewhere to be used for making of tight cask, who shall cast bye all such as they shall judge not merchantable both in respect of worm-holes and due assize viz that are not in length four foot & half, in breadth three inches and half without sap, in thickness three quraters of an inch, & not more or lesse then an eight part of an inch then three quarters thick: well, and even hewed and sufficient for that use. And they or some one of the shall at all times upon request give attendance; & they shall enter in a book the number of all such merchantable Pipe-staves as they shall approve, and for whom.

And if any man shall put aboard any Ship, or other vessel any Pipe-staves other then shall be so searched and approved, to the end to be transported to any part of Spain or Portugal, except they should be shipped for dry cask, he shall forfeit the same whole parcell or the value therof; and the said Viewers shall be allowed two shillings for everie thousand of Pipe-staves which they shall so search, as well the refuse as the merchantable, to be paid by him that sets them a work.

And if any Master or other Officer of any Ship, or other vessel shall receive into such Ship or vessel any parcel of Pipe-staves to be transported into any of the said Dominions which shall not be searched, and allowed as merchantable, and so certified by a note under the hand of one of the said Viewers such Master shall forfeit for everie thousand

Poor.

It ordered by this Court and Authoritie therof; that any Shire Court, or any two Magistrates out of Court shall have power to determin all differences about lawfull setling, and providing for poor persons; and shall have power to dispose of all unsetled persons into such towns as they shall judge to be most fit for the maintainance, and imployment of such persons and families, for the ease of the Countrie. [1639] * * *

[*49] Strangers.

It is ordered by this Court and the Authoritie therof; that no Town or person shal receive any stranger resorting hither with intent to reside in this Jurisdiction, nor shall allow any Lot or Habitation to any, or entertain any such above three weeks, except such person shall have allowance under the hand of some one Magistrate, upon pain of everie Town that shall give, or sell any Lot or Habitation to any not so licenced such Fine to the Countrie as that County Court shall impose, not exceeding fifty pounds, nor lesse then ten pounds. And of everie person receiving any such for longer time then is heer expressed or allowed, in some special cases as before, or in case of entertainment of friends resorting from other parts of this Country in amitie with us, shall forfeit as aforesaid, not exceeding twenty pounds, nor lesse then four pounds: and for everie month after so offending, shal forfeit as aforesaid not exceeding ten pounds, nor lesse then fourty shillings. Also, that all Constables shall inform the Courts of new commers which they know to be admitted without licence, from time to time. [1637 1638 1647] See Fugitives, Lib. com: Tryalls. *** Suits, vexatious suits.

It is ordered and decreed, and by this Court declared; that in all Cases where it appears to the Court that the Plaintiffe hath willingly & wittingly done wrong to the Defendant in commencing and prosecuting any Action, Suit, Complaint or Indictment in his own name or in the name of others, he shall pay treble damages to the partie greived, and be fined fourty shillings to the Common Treasurie. [1641 1646]

Swyne.

It is ordered by this Court, and by the Authoritie therof; that every Township within this Jurisdiction shall henceforth have power, and are heerby required from time to time to make Orders for preventing all harms by swine in corn, meadow, pastures and gardens; as also to impose penalties according to their best discretion: and to appoint one of their Inhabitants by Warrent under the hands of the Select-men, or the Constable where no Select-men are, to levie all such Fines and Penalties by them in that case imposed (if the Town neglect it).

And where Towns border each upon other, whose Orders may be various, satisfaction shall be made accrding to the Orders of that Town where the damage is done.

But if the swine be sufficiently ringed and yoaked, as the Orders of the Town to which they belong doeth require, then where no fence is, or that it be insufficient through which the swine come to trespasse, the Owner of the land or fence shall bear all damages. * * *

[*50] Tobacco.

This Court finding that since the repealing of the former Laws against Tobacco, the same is more abused then before doth therfore order,

That no man shall take any tobacco within twenty poles of any house, or so neer as may indanger the same, or neer any Barn, corn, or hay-cock as may occasion the fyring therof, upon pain of ten shillings for everie such offence, besides full recompence of all damages done by means therof. Nor shall any take tobacco in any Inne or common Victualing-house, except in a private room there, so as neither the Master of the said house nor any other Guests there shall take offence therat, which if any doe, then such person shall forthwith forbear, upon pain of two shillings sixpence for everie such offence. And for all Fines incurred by this Law, one half part shall be to the Informer the other to the poor of the town where the offence is done. [1638 1647]

Torture

It is ordered, decreed, and by this Court declared; that no man shall be forced by torture to confesse any crime against himselfe or any other, unles it be in some Capital case, where he is first fully convicted by clear and sufficient evidence to be guilty. After which, if the Case be of that nature that it is very apparent there be other Conspirators or Confoederates with him; then he may be tortured, yet not with such tortures as be barbarous and inhumane.

2 And that no man shall be beaten with above fourty stripes for one Fact at one time. Nor shall any man be punished with whipping, except he have not othewise to answer the Law, unles his crime be very shamefull, and his course of life vitious and profligate. [1641]

Source: Le Projet Albion/Puritan Studies on the Web/Primary Sources

http://puritanism.online.fr/puritanism/sources/lawslibertyes1648.html

Appendix F
TRANSCRIPTION OF THE CHARTER OF 1650

The Charter of the President and Fellows of Harvard College under the seal of the Colony of Massachusetts Bay and bearing the date May 31st A.D.1650

Whereas through the good hand of God many well devoted persons have been and daily are moved and stirred up to give and bestow sundry gifts legacies lands and revenues for the advancement of all good literature arts and sciences in Harvard College in Cambridge in the County of Middlesex and to the maintenance of the President and Fellows and for all accommodations of buildings and all other necessary provisions that may conduce to the education of the English and Indian youth of this country in knowledge and godliness. **It is** therefore ordered and enacted by this Court and the authority thereof that for the furthering of so good a work and for the purposes aforesaid from henceforth that the said College in Cambridge in Middlesex in New England shall be a Corporation consisting of seven persons (to wit) a President five Fellows and a Treasurer or Bursar and that Henry Dunster shall be the first President Samuel Mather Samuel Danforth Masters of Arts Jonathan Mitchell Comfort Starr and Samuel Eaton Bachelors of Arts shall be the five Fellows and Thomas Danforth to be present Treasurer all of them being inhabitants in the Bay and shall be the first seven persons of which the said Corporation shall consist And that the said seven persons or the greater number of them procuring the presence of the Overseers of the College and by their counsel and consent shall have power and are hereby authorized at any time or times to elect a new President Fellows or Treasurer so oft and from time to time as any of the said person or persons shall die or be removed which said President and Fellows for the time being shall for ever hereafter in name and fact be one body politic and corporate in law to all intents and purposes and shall have perpetual succession And shall be called by the name of President and Fellows of Harvard College And shall from time to time be eligible as aforesaid. And by that name they and their successors shall and may purchase and acquire to themselves or take and receive upon free-gift and donation any lands tenements or hereditaments within this jurisdiction of the Massachusetts not exceeding the value of five hundred pounds per annum and any goods and sums of money whatsoever to the use and behoof of the said President Fellows and scholars of the said College and also may sue and plead or be sued and impleaded by the name aforesaid in all Courts and places of judicature within the jurisdiction aforesaid and that the said President with any three of the Fellows shall have power and are hereby authorized when they shall think fit to make and appoint a common seal for the use of the said Corporation. And the President and Fellows or the major part of them from time to time may meet and choose such officers and servants for the College and make such allowance to them and them also to remove and after death or removal to choose such others and to make from time to time such orders and by-laws for the better ordering and carrying on the work of the College as they shall think fit. Provided the said orders be allowed by the Overseers. And also that the President and Fellows or major part of them with the Treasurer shall have power to make conclusive bargains for lands and tenements to be purchased by the said Corporation for valuable considerations. **And** for the better ordering of the government of the said College and Corporation be it enacted by the authority aforesaid that the President and three more of the Fellows shall and may from time to time upon due warning or notice

APPENDIX F

given by the President to the rest hold a meeting for the debating and concluding of affairs concerning the profits and revenues of any lands and disposing of their goods. Provided that all the said disposings be according to the will of the donors. And for direction in all emergent occasions execution of all orders and by-laws and for the procuring of a general meeting of all the Overseers and society in great and difficult cases and in cases of non-agreement. In all which cases aforesaid the conclusion shall be made by the major part the said President having a casting voice the Overseers consenting thereunto. And that all the aforesaid transactions shall tend to and for the use and behoof of the President Fellows scholars and officers of the said College and for all accommodations of buildings books and all other necessary provisions and furnitures as may be for the advancement and education of youth in all manner of good literature arts and sciences. **And** further be it ordered by this Court and the authority thereof that all the lands tenements or hereditaments houses or revenues within this jurisdiction to the aforesaid President or College appertaining not exceeding the value of five hundred pounds per annum shall from henceforth be freed from all civil impositions taxes and rates all goods to the said corporation or to any scholars thereof appertaining shall be exempted from all manner of toll customs and excise whatsoever. And that the said President Fellows and scholars together with the servants and other necessary officers to the said President or College appertaining not exceeding ten, viz. three to the President and seven to the College belonging shall be exempted from all personal civil offices military exercises or services watchings and wardings and such of their estates not exceeding one hundred pounds a man shall be free from all country taxes or rates whatsoever and none others.

In witness whereof the Court hath caused the seal of the colony to be hereunto affixed. Dated the one and thirtieth day of the third month called May. Anno 1650.

THOMAS DUDLEY Governor.

TRANSCRIPTION OF THE CHARTER OF 1650

Source: Harvard Library: https://guides.library.harvard.edu/c.php?g=880222&p=6323072

Appendix G
HARVARD MOTTO 1692

The motto of the University adopted in 1692 was "Veritas Christo et Ecclesiae," which translated from Latin means "Truth for Christ and the Church." This phrase was embedded on a shield and can be found on many buildings around campus including the Widener library, Memorial Church, and various dorms in Harvard Yard. Interestingly, the top two books on the shield are face up while the bottom book is face down. This symbolizes the limits of reason, and the need for God's revelation. With the secularization of the school, the current shield now contains only the word "Veritas" with three open books.

Source: Harvard Christian Fellowship at http://www.hcs.harvard.edu/~gsascf/shield-and-veritas-history/

Appendix H
THE LAWS OF HARVARD COLLEGE (1767)

CHAP. II

Of a religious and virtuous Life

I All Persons of what Degree soever residing at the College, and all Undergraduates whether dwelling in the College or in the Town, shall constantly and seasonably attend the Worship of God in the Chapel Morning and Evening; and if any Undergraduate comes to Prayers after the Exercises are begun (without Reasons allowed by the President or the Tutor that calls over the weekly Bill) he shall be fined one Penny each time—and if he is absent from Prayers (without Reasons as aforesaid) he shall be fined two Pence for every such Neglect.

II All the Scholars shall at Sun-set in the Evening preceding the Lord's Day, lay aside all their Diversions, and retire to their Chambers, and not unnecessarily leave them; and all Disorders on said Evening shall be punished as Violations of the Sabbath are. And every Scholar shall on the Lord's Day carefully apply himself to the Duties of Religion—and whoever shall profane said Day by unnecessary [5] Business, or Visiting, or walking on the Common, or in the Streets or Fields of the Town of Cambridge, or shall use any Diversions, or otherwise behave himself disorderly or unbecoming the Season, shall be fined not exceeding three shillings.

APPENDIX H

[And if such a Scholar shall not reform after being privately admonished, he shall receive a public Admonition, or be punished by Degradation or Rustication.]

III If any Scholar shall be absent from the public Worship on either Part of the Lord's Day, or upon public Fasts or Thanksgivings without offering a sufficient Reason, before the Ringing of the second Bell, if the case will allow it, to the President or one of the Tutors, he shall be fined not exceeding two Shillings—and if any Scholar come to public Worship after the Exercise is begun, he shall be fined not exceeding eight Pence—And whoever shall be guilty of irreverent or indecent Behaviour at the public Worship, or on any part of the Days of public Fasting or Thanksgiving, he shall be fined not exceeding two shillings or otherwise according to the Aggravation of the Offence. [6]

IV That proper Care may be taken that all the Scholars duly attend the public Worship of God, it is ordered, that, every Undergraduate above one & twenty Years of Age; who shall propose to attend statedly on the Service of the Church of England, shall signify in writing his Desire to the President & Tutors. And that every Undergraduate under the Age of one & twenty Years, who shall propose to attend the said Service, shall bring to the President a written Request from his Parent or Guardian that he may attend said Service; & all Undergraduates who shall not produce such Writing shall be obliged to attend the congregational Worship as heretofore.

V No Undergraduate shall go to the Place of public Worship before the Ringing of the second Bell; and whoever shall transgress this Law, shall be fined not exceeding one shilling.

VI [Undergraduates shall in their Course repeat at least the Heads of the Forenoon & Afternoon Sermons on the Lord's Day Evenings in the Chapel; & such as are delinquent shall be fined not exceeding one shilling.]

[7]

VII All indecent or irreverent Behaviour at Prayers or public Lectures shall be punished not exceeding two shillings.

THE LAWS OF HARVARD COLLEGE (1767)

VIII All Scholars shall shew due Respect & Honor to all that are in the Government & Instruction of the College; particularly, Undergraduates shall be uncovered in the College Yard, when any of the Overseers, the President, or Fellows of the Corporation, or any others concerned in the Government or Instruction of the College are therein; and Bachelors of Arts shall be uncovered when the President is there. And whoever shall offend against this Law, shall be punished not exceeding two shillings.

IX No Scholar that is on Mr Hollis's Foundation or that receives any other Benefit from the College, shall enjoy the same any longer than he continues exemplary for Sobriety, Diligence, & good order.

Source: Colonial Society of Massachusetts

https://www.colonialsociety.org/node/432

Appendix I
HARVARD PRESIDENT SAMUEL LANGDON 1775

Samuel Langdon was a colonial chaplain and pastor before being chosen as President of Harvard in 1776.

In an Election Day address, May 31, 1775, Langdon spoke to the Massachusetts Provincial Congress:

> We have rebelled against God. We have lost the true spirit of Christianity, though we retain the outward profession and form of it.
>
> We have neglected and set light by the glorious Gospel of our Lord Jesus Christ and His holy commands and institutions.
>
> The worship of many is but mere compliment to the Deity, while their hearts are far from Him. By many, the Gospel is corrupted into a superficial system of moral philosophy, little better than ancient Platonism....
>
> My brethren, let us repent and implore the divine mercy. Let us amend our ways and our doings, reform everything that has been provoking the Most High, and thus endeavor to obtain the gracious interpositions of providence for our deliverance...
>
> May the Lord hear us in this day of trouble...
>
> We will rejoice in His salvation, and in the name of our God, we will set up our banners!...

HARVARD PRESIDENT SAMUEL LANGDON 1775

> Wherefore is all this evil upon us? Is it not because we have forsaken the Lord?
>
> Can we say we are innocent of crimes against God? No, surely it becomes us to humble ourselves under His mighty hand, that He may exalt us in due time....
>
> My brethren, let us repent and implore the divine mercy.
>
> Let us amend our ways and our doings, reform everything that has been provoking the Most High, and thus endeavor to obtain the gracious interpositions of Providence for our deliverance ...
>
> If God be for us, who can be against us? The enemy has reproached us for calling on His name and professing our trust in Him.
>
> They have made a mock of our solemn fasts and every appearance of serious Christianity in the land....
>
> May our land be purged from all its sins!
>
> Then the Lord will be our refuge and our strength, a very present help in trouble, and we will have no reason to be afraid, though thousands of enemies set themselves against us round about.
>
> May the Lord hear us in this day of trouble.... We will rejoice in His salvation, and in the name of our God, we will set up our banners.

Source: Belcher Foundation
https://www.belcherfoundation.org/government_corrupted.htm

After being president of Harvard, Langdon was a delegate to the New Hampshire Convention which ratified the United States Constitution in 1788. There Langdon gave an address "The Republic of the Israelites an Example to the American States."

> The Israelites may be considered as a pattern to the world in all ages, and from them we may learn what will exalt our character, and what will depress and bring us to ruin.
>
> Let us therefore look over their constitution and laws, enquire into their practice, and observe how their

APPENDIX I

prosperity . . . depended on their strict observance of the divine commands both as to their government and religion.

Source: Consource.org

https://www.consource.org/document/the-republic-of-the-israelites-an-example-to-the-american-states-by-samuel-langdon-1788-6-5/

BIBLIOGRAPHY

Allen, J.H. *The Unitarian Movement Since the Reformation.* New York: Christian Literature Co., 1894.

Baumer, Franklin L. *Religion and the Rise of Scepticism.* New York: Harcourt, Brace, & Co., 1960.

Bellamy, Joseph. *A Careful and Strict Examination of the External Covenant, and of the Principles by Which It Is Supported. A Reply to the Rev. Mr. Moses Mather's Piece, Entitled, The Visible Church in Covenant with God, Further Illustrated, &c. A Vindication of the Plan on Which the Churches in New-England Were Originally Formed. Interspersed with Remarks upon Some Things, Advanced by Mr. Sandeman, on Some of the Important Points in Debate.* New-Haven: Thomas and Samuel Green, 1770.

Bellamy, Joseph. *An essay on the nature and glory of the Gospel of Jesus Christ: as also on the nature and consequences of spiritual blindness: and the nature and effects of Divine illumination. Designed as a supplement to the author's letters and dialogues on the nature of love to God, faith in Christ, and assurance of a title to eternal life.* Boston, N.E.: S. Kneeland, in Queen-Street, opposite to the probate office, 1762.

Bellamy, Joseph. *The Inconsistence of Renouncing the Half-Way Covenant, and Yet Retaining the Half-Way Practice. A Dialogue.* New-Haven: Thomas and Samuel Green, 1769.

Bellamy, Joseph. *The Millennium, or, the thousand years of prosperity, promised to the church of God, in the Old Testament and in the New, shortly to commence, and to be carried on to perfection, under the auspices of him, who in the vision, was presented to St. John.* Elizabeth Town (Elizabeth, N.J.): Shepard Kollock, 1794.

Bellamy, Joseph. *Theron, Paulinus, and Aspasio. Or, Letters and dialogues, upon the nature of love to God, faith in Christ, assurance of a title to eternal life. Containing some remarks on the sentiments of the Revd. Messieurs Hervey and Marshal, on these subjects.* Boston: S. Kneeland, opposite to the probate-office in Queen-Street, 1759.

Bellamy, Joseph. *True religion delineated; or, Experimental religion, as distinguished from formality on the one hand, and enthusiasm on the other,*

BIBLIOGRAPHY

set in a scriptural and rational light. In two discourses. In which some of the principal errors both of the Arminians and Antinomians are confuted, the foundation and superstructure of their different schemes demolished, and the truth as it is in Jesus, explained and proved. The whole adapted to the weakest capacities, and designed for the establishment, comfort and quickening of the people of God, in these evil times. Boston: S. Kneeland, Queen-Street, 1750.

Bercovitch, Sacvan, ed., *Jeremiads: A Library of American Puritan Writings, The Seventeenth Century*. New York: AMS Press, Inc., 1985.

Boardman, George Nye. *A History of New England Theology*. New York: A.D.F. Randolph Co. 1899.

Chauncy, Charles. *Seasonable Thoughts on the State of Religion in New-England*. Boston: Rogers and Fowle, 1743.

Clap, Thomas. *The Annals or History of Yale-College: in New Haven, in the Colony of Connecticut, from the First Founding Thereof, in the Year 1700, to the Year 1766: with an Appendix, Containing the Present State of the Colleges, the Method of Instruction and Government, with the Officers, Benefactors and Graduates*. New-Haven: printed for John Hotchkiss and B. Mecom, 1766.

Clarke, Dorus. *Orthodox Congregationalism and the Sects*. Boston: Lee and Shepard, 1871.

Cotton, John. *God's Promise to His Plantation*. London, 1630.

Crawford, Michael J. *Seasons of Grace: Colonial New England's Revival Tradition in Its British Context*. Oxford: Oxford University Press, 1991.

De Jong, Peter Y. *The Covenant Idea in New England Theology 1620–1847*. Grand Rapids: Wm. B. Eerdmans, 1945.

Dexter, Henry Martyn. *The Congregationalism of the Last Three Hundred Years, as Seen in its Literature with Special Reference to Certain Recondite, Neglected, or Disputed Passages: in Twelve Lectures, Delivered on the Southworth Foundation in the Theological Seminary at Andover, Mass., 1876–1879: with a Bibliographical Appendix*. New York: Harper, 1880.

Edwards, Jonathan. *The great concern of a watchman for souls, appearing in the duty he has to do, and the account he has to give, represented & improved, in a sermon preach'd at the ordination of the Reverend Mr. Jonathan Judd, to the pastoral office over the Church of Christ, in the new precinct at Northampton, June, 8, 1743*. Boston: Green, Bushell, and Alen, for N. Procter, at the Bible and Dove in Ann-Street, near the draw-bridge, 1753.

Foster, Frank Hugh. *A Genetic History of the New England Theology*. Chicago: University of Chicago Press, 1907.

Gaustad, Edwin Scott. *The Great Awakening*. New York: Harper & Brothers, New York, 1957.

Goen, C.C. *Revivalism and Separatism in New England, 1740–1800: Strict Congregationalists and Separate Baptists in the Great Awakening*. New Haven: Yale University Press, 1962.

BIBLIOGRAPHY

Haroutunian, Joseph. *Piety Versus Moralism: The Passing of the New England Theology.* New York: Henry Holt, 1932.

Harrington, Michael. *The Politics at God's Funeral: The Spiritual Crisis of Western Civilization.* New York: Holt, Rinehart, and Winston, 1983

Heimert. Alan and Miller, Perry, eds. *The Great Awakening: Documents Illustrating the Crisis and Its Consequences.* New York: The Bobbs-Merrill Company, Inc., 1967.

Hopkins, Samuel. *An address to the people of New-England. Representing the very great importance of attaching the Indians to their interest; not only by treating them justly and kindly; but by using proper endeavors to settle Christianity among them.* Philadelphia: Reprinted by B. Franklin, and D. Hall, 1757.

Hopkins, Samuel. *A Treatise on the Millennium.* Boston: Isaiah Thomas and Ebenezer T. Andrews, MDCCXCIII (1793).

Kuklick, Bruce, ed. *American Religious Thought of the 18th and 19th Centuries.* New York: Garland Publishing, Inc., 1987.

Lovejoy, David. S. *Religious Enthusiasm in the New World.* Cambridge, Mass.: Harvard University Press, 1985.

Marini, Stephen A. *Radical Sects of Revolutionary New England.* Cambridge: Harvard University Press, 1982.

Mather, Increase. *Ratio Discipline Fratrum Nov-Anglorum: A Faithful Account of the Discipline Professed and Practiced in the Church of New-England, With Interspersed and Instructive Reflections on the Discipline of the Primitive Churches.* Boston: S. Gerrish in Cornhill, 1726.

Mayhew, Jonathan. *A Defence of the Observation on the Charter and Conduct of the Society for Propagating the Gospel in Foreign Parts Against an Anonymous Pamphlet Falsely Intitled, A Candid Examination of Dr. Mayhew's Observations, &c. and also against the Letter to a Friend Annexed Thereto, Said to Contain a Short Vindication of the Said Society. By One of its Members.* Boston: Printed and sold by R. and S. Draper, in Newburty Street; Edes and Gill, in Queen-Street; and T. & J. Fleet, in Cornhill, 1763.

Miller, Perry, and Johnson, Thomas, eds. *The Puritans: A Sourcebook of Their Writings.* New York: Harper Torchbooks, 1963

Moe, Alfred K. *A History of Harvard.* Cambridge, Mass.: Harvard University Press, 1896.

Morgan, Edmund S., ed. *Puritan Political Ideas.* Indianapolis: Bobbs-Merrill, 1965.

Morison, Samuel Eliot. *Three Centuries of Harvard.* Cambridge, Mass.: Belknap Press. 1936.

Morse, Jedidiah. *Review of American Unitarianism.* Boston: Samuel T. Armstrong, 1815.

Nelson, John Oliver. *The Rise of the Princeton Theology: A Genetic Study of American Presbyterianism until 1850.* Ann Arbor: University Microfilms, 1976 (dissertation, Yale University, 1935).

BIBLIOGRAPHY

Pencak, William. *War, Politics, and Revolution in Provincial Massachusetts.* Boston: Northeastern University Press, 1981.

Pierce, Benjamin. *A History of Harvard University.* Cambridge, Mass.: Brown Shattuck and Co., 1833 (handwritten Harvard archives).

Pope, Earl A. *New England Calvinism and Disruption of the Presbyterian Church.* New York: Garland, 1987

Quincy, Josiah. *A History of Harvard University.* Boston: Crosby, Nichols, Lee, & Co., 1860.

Records of the Overseers of Harvard University (handwritten Harvard archives)

Sprague, William B. *Lectures on Revivals of Religion* 2d ed. New York, 1833.

Story, Thomas. *A Journal of the Life of Thomas Story.* Newcastle-upon-Tyne: Isaac Thompson and Co., 1747.

Taylor, Nathanael. *A discourse of the nature and necessity of faith in Jesus Christ: with an answer to the pleas of our modern Unitarians for the sufficiency of bare morality or mere charity to salvation.* London: printed by R.R. for John Lawrence, and Thomas Cockerill, 1700.

Taylor, Nathanael. *A preservative against deism: Shewing the great advantage of revelation above reason, in the two great points, pardon of sin, and a future state of happiness. With an appendix in answer to a letter of A.W. against Revealed Religion, in the Oracles of Reason.* London: John Lawrence, 1698.

Thomas, M.H., ed., *The Diary of Samuel Sewall.* New York: Farrar, Straus and Giroux, 1973.

Tyerman, Luke. *Life of George Whitefield.* London: Hodder and Stoughton, 1877.

Walker, Williston. *The Creeds and Platforms of Congregationalism.* New York: Charles Scribner's Sons, 1893.

Vidich, Arthur J. and Lyman, Stanford M. *American Sociology: Worldly Rejections of Religion and Their Directions.* New Haven: Yale University Press, 1985

Waters, Thomas Franklin. *Ipswhich in The Massachusetts Bay Colony.* Ipswich, Mass.: The Ipswich Historical Society, 1917.

Wertenbaker, Thomas Jefferson. *The Puritan Oligarchy: The Founding of American Civilization.* New York: Charles Scribner's Sons, 1947.

White, John. *The Planter's Pea.* London: William Iones, 1630.

Whitefield, George. *A Vindication and Confirmation of the Remarkable Work of God in New-England.* London, 1742.

Wilbur, Earl Morse. *A History of Unitarianism: Socinianism and Its Antecedents.* Cambridge: Harvard University, 1945.

Williams, Elisha. *The Essential Rights and Liberties of Protestants. A Seasonable Plea for the Liberty of Conscience, and the Right or Private Judgment.* Boston, 1744.

Williams, George Huntston. *The Harvard Divinity School: Its Place in Harvard University and in American Culture.* Boston: The Beacon Press, 1954.

Wright, Conrad. *The Beginnings of Unitarianism in America.* Boston: Beacon Press, 1955.

www.ingramcontent.com/pod-product-compliance
Lightning Source LLC
Chambersburg PA
CBHW070924160426
43193CB00011B/1575